CU01456029

# A.P. 'Bunny' Lucas
## The Best of All My Boys

**David Pracy**

**With a foreword by Robin Hobbs**

First published in Great Britain by
Association of Cricket Statisticians and Historians
Cardiff CF11 9XR
© ACS, 2010

British Library Cataloguing-in-Publication Data.
A catalogue record for this book is available from the British Library.

ISBN: 978 1 905138 84 5
Typeset by Limlow Books

# Contents

*... feet in front of the bat, and a little pointed forward ...*

# *Foreword*
## *By Robin Hobbs*

I've been very fortunate to have lived in the lovely area of Fryerning for over 35 years, and to have played professional cricket for my county of Essex. Ever since I was a small boy, my interest in the past history of Essex cricketers has been high, and it remains so to this day.

It was by chance that in 1975, I bought a cottage that just happened to be opposite Barn Mead, where C.J.Kortright, the great fast bowler lived for a number of years. I can walk across the fields to Fryerning Church where he and A.P.Lucas are buried almost twenty-two yards apart, in accordance with their wishes when alive, as they were lifelong friends.

Much has been written about Kortright, but very little in relation to Lucas. When I first located his grave many years ago, it was hardly visible, as it was completely overgrown and had not been tended for years. This I thought was a pitiful epitaph for somebody who had given so much to cricket, and who was a churchwarden for over twenty years at Fryerning. So each spring, I clean it up, and cut down the brambles around his grave, so people who visit the churchyard may stop and ponder for a while on the last resting place of one of England's great unsung heroes. It echoes of the great men of that time who played against Lucas such as Grace, Spofforth, and Morley, just to name a few.

David Pracy's book on the life of Bunny, as he was known, will be of immense interest to lovers of the 'Golden Age' of cricket, thoroughly researched, and written with great thought. One can only hope a lot of younger cricketers, and followers of our great game, will take an interest in past players who did so much to form the basis of Essex cricket over a hundred years ago. I have no doubt that, had he been given the exposure by the media of cricket in our age, Bunny Lucas would have been a sporting super star.

Fryerning, Essex
January 2010

# *Introduction*

In the short story *A Long–Ago Affair*,[1] John Galsworthy's landscape painter Herbert Marsland returns in 1921 to a cricket ground where he played as a boy, and finds that it had been turned into a golf course:

> Thirty-nine years ago – his sixteenth birthday. How vividly he remembered his new pads! A.P.Lucas had played against them and only made thirty-two – one founded one's style on A.P.Lucas in those days – feet in front of the bat, and pointed a little forward, elegant; you never saw it now, and a good thing too – one could sacrifice too much for style! Still, the tendency was all the other way; style was too much 'off', perhaps!

Galsworthy, a great cricket-lover, was the same age as his character, and Alfred Perry Lucas was one of his boyhood heroes.[2] His discussion of style was referring to far more than cricket, but it may explain why Lucas has to some extent been forgotten: though regarded by his contemporaries as among the finest of defensive batsmen, his strengths perhaps went out of fashion.

Lucas was educated at Uppingham School in Rutland, where his cricket coach was the old Surrey player H.H.Stephenson, who was appointed in 1872. The influence of Stephenson was immediate and lasting. When he arrived, the exceptionally gifted C.E.Green had been the only Uppingham man to play first-class cricket, but within five years the powerful Cambridge University team contained five of them – the highest number ever provided by a single school. They were W.S.Patterson, H.T.Luddington, S.S.Schultz, D.Q.Steel and Lucas.

All went on to play first-class cricket for other sides after university, but Stephenson regarded Lucas as 'the best of all my boys'. At the end of his life he would mutter: 'Yes, straight to meet her, middle of the bat, like those early boys of mine, who listened to what I said to them. Do you remember Lucas?' And the pupil respected his teacher. His obituary in *The Times* recorded that 'Mr Lucas had been carefully coached at Uppingham by H.H.Stephenson – he was by far the best of Stephenson's pupils – and throughout his career he never tired of saying how much he owed to his teacher.'

Lucas was known to his friends as 'Bunny', which was quite a common nickname among public school boys. Its first recorded application to him

---

1    *Caravan: The Collected Stories of John Galsworthy,* Heinemann, 1925, p 687.
2    Marrot, H.V., *The Life and Letters of John Galsworthy,* Heinemann, 1935, p 35.

was in 1877 when he was playing for the Uppingham Rovers, a wandering team of former pupils at the school. He was their star player, and it was probably they that gave him the name. His contemporaries never referred to him as Alfred but always by his initials or his nickname; when needing to distinguish him from other Lucases, I have followed suit.

In a first-class career that spanned 34 years, Lucas played in some of the greatest and most controversial matches of his age. He assisted England, the Gentlemen, Cambridge University, MCC, Surrey, Middlesex and finally Essex, where his role in the achievement of first-class status was vital. He was also a jobber on the London Stock Exchange and a lifelong member of the Church of England, latterly as a churchwarden in the Essex village of Fryerning, where he made his home. His long and varied cricket career and his life outside the game are well worth revisiting.

# Chapter One
## *The Lucas family*

John Arlott wrote of the prolific and versatile author and critic E.V.Lucas that 'his cricket writing has charm and distinction and, simultaneously, carries conviction.'[3] Lucas in turn wrote: 'One of my greatest griefs, which has followed me all my life, has been to answer "No" to the question "Are you related to A.P. Lucas?"'[4] Any cricket-loving namesake would have been disappointed at being unable to claim kinship with him, but it is not surprising that they were unrelated, for the surname Lucas is fairly common in southern and central England. It is the earliest form of the personal name Luke, or 'bright and shining one', and simply indicates a descendent of a man called Lucas.[5]

A.P.Lucas was born on 20 February 1857 at 22 Chesham Place, Westminster, part of the Lowndes Estate in the fashionable Central London parish of St George's, Hanover Square. The neighbours included Lord John Russell, Viscount Castlereagh and the Bishops of London and Salisbury.

The Lucases were a comfortable, upper middle class family, descended from a long line of East Anglian gentry who could trace their origins back to the twelfth century, and who had sometimes moved in royal circles.[6] In 1180 a man called Lucas held land from the Abbey of Bury St Edmunds, where his descendants filled the offices of alderman and bailiff. After some two centuries, Lucas became the family's hereditary surname and in 1359, Edmund Lucas married Elizabeth, sister of Sir Thomas Morieux, Constable of the Tower. Their great-great-grandson, Thomas Lucas (c1470-1531), became a privy counsellor and Solicitor-General to King Henry VII. He bought and united the three Suffolk manors of Little Saxham, and took personal charge of building a massive and splendid hall. Thomas's great-great-grandson William (d 1640) married the daughter of Robert Gibson, an alderman of Norwich, and Gibson was to be a forename popular in the Lucas family for over two centuries.

The first Gibson Lucas (1615-1698) was among the gentry appointed by parliament in 1643 to a standing committee for the Eastern Counties, in which Cromwell was second-in-command. His cousin, Sir Charles Lucas,

---

3    Introduction to *Cricket All His Life: The Cricket Writings of E.V.Lucas,* Pavilion, 1989.
4    E.V.Lucas, *Reading, Writing and Remembering: A Literary Record*, Methuen, 1932, p vii.
5    P.H.Reaney and R.M.Wilson, *A Dictionary of English Surnames* [Revised Edition], Oxford University Press, 1997.
6    This chapter is based mainly on J.J.Howard (ed), *The Visitation of Suffolke: Volume 2*, Samuel Timms, 1871.

was on the other side in the Civil War: he played a leading part in the Royalist seizure of Colchester Castle in 1648, and was shot without trial after Parliamentary forces recaptured it. Gibson's great-grandson, Gibson Lucas III (1732-1790), Bunny's great-grandfather, became lord of the manor of Filby, six miles north-west of Yarmouth. All Saints' Church at Filby contains memorial tablets and stained glass windows to several members of the Lucas family.

In the nineteenth century, the Lucases were at the heart of an influential network of gentry and clerical families in a group of small, remote parishes in the hundred of East Flegg on the Norfolk coast.[7] Gibson Lucas IV (1768-1848) was the chief owner, lord of the manor, patron and incumbent of Filby, and in 1798 he married Mary Anne Salmon (1778-1846). Her father, Benjamin Wymberley Salmon, was rector of three of the parishes, and was appointed domestic chaplain to the Prince of Wales (afterwards George IV) in 1805.

Gibson Lucas IV had four sons, of whom the third, Orton, was Bunny's father. The eldest son, the fifth and last Gibson in the line, did not inherit the estate, but became Rector of St Lawrence, Southampton. His son, Bunny's cousin Charles Frank Lucas, was a right-handed bat and excellent long-stop who, from 1864 to 1880, played fourteen matches for Hampshire and three for the Gentlemen of the South, as well as many non-first-class games for the Gentlemen of Hampshire. His finest performance was in Hampshire's ten-wicket win against Surrey in 1866, when he opened the innings and was last out for 135 in a total of 281.

After Gibson Lucas IV's death, his second son, Charles Lucas (1804-1889), became lord of the manor, patron and rector of Filby, where in 1873 he owned 1,543 acres. In 1836 William White described Filby as 'a small parish and straggling village'; nowadays it is a popular holiday place, with boating and wildlife among the attractions. In 1848 Charles married Frances Belgrave, daughter of the Rector of Preston, near Uppingham. Their son, Percy Montagu, was the father of Percy Belgrave 'Laddie' Lucas, the well-known golfer, writer, Conservative MP, World War II fighter pilot and brother-in-law of Douglas Bader, whose biography he wrote. Bunny and Laddie Lucas were therefore first cousins once removed. One of Laddie Lucas's golf partners was Leonard Crawley, who between the wars won the Amateur Championship, played in four Walker Cup sides and 97 internationals, and played cricket for Worcestershire and Essex.[8]

Gibson IV's youngest son, William Salmon Lucas (1817-1857), was the father of Arthur (1851-1921), Bunny's cousin and perhaps the closest to him of the extended Lucas family. Evidently academically gifted, Arthur won an exhibition to Uppingham School, where in 1870 he was in the

---

7    This paragraph based mostly on William White's Norfolk directories for 1836 and 1845.
8    See *Dictionary of National Biography* entries for Laddie Lucas and Crawley.

cricket eleven with Bunny's brother Philip,[9] and another to Clare College Cambridge, where he obtained his BA in 1874. In the following year he took holy orders and Bunny arrived at Clare. In 1885 Arthur assisted at Bunny's wedding and, as a master at Tonbridge School, introduced him to Charles Kortright, who was to become one of the fastest bowlers of all time and a lifelong friend of Bunny.

Orton Lucas was born at Great Yarmouth in 1808. He was a solicitor who had his own practice at Trafalgar Square in 1841, when he was also described in the census as being of independent means. By 1852 he was a partner in the firm of Fisher and Lucas at 50 Fenchurch Street in the City of London: he became senior partner in what seems to have been a lucrative practice.

In 1839 Orton married Mary Rachel Salmon, so Bunny's parents were first cousins. Her father, William Orton Salmon (1779-1828), was the brother of Orton Lucas's mother Mary Ann. He entered the service of the East India Company and in 1803 married Elizabeth Frederica Potts at Kanpur.[10] In 1808 he obtained the important post of Collector of Benares, where Mary Rachel was born in 1815. A year later, with the patronage of Lord Hastings, he was appointed president of the Board of Revenue of Central India. In 1824 ill health forced him to return to England, but he never fully recovered and died in 1828.

Bunny was the youngest of six children, four boys and two girls. It may well have been because of the connection with the Belgrave family that Orton Lucas sent his sons to Uppingham, rather than one of the more established public schools. His being able to afford the fees for all four boys, rather than just the eldest (as was the case in some families), indicates that he was pretty well-off.

Of Bunny's siblings, **William Orton Lucas** was born in 1844 and baptised at his grandfather's church in Filby. In the 1861 census he was listed as a boarder at Uppingham and in 1863 he became school cricket captain. He won an exhibition to Exeter College, Oxford where he obtained a BA in 1867 and an MA in 1870. He took holy orders and in the 1871 census was described as 'curate without charge of souls, acting assistant master at Uppingham School.' Poor health prevented his continuing in the post and he died in 1874, aged only thirty.

**Eliza**, born in 1847, and **Fanny Margaret**, born in 1855, never married. They are listed in censuses as scholars and no governess is mentioned so they probably went to school, but I haven't found out which. Like William, Fanny died young, in 1884 aged only 29. Eliza remained at home with her mother. The last surviving sibling, she died at Cheshunt, Hertfordshire in 1937, aged 90.

---

9     Details of all Uppingham careers and other background information about the school from *Uppingham School Roll: 1853–1947*, H.F.W.Deane, 1948.

10    Obituary in *The Oriental Herald and Journal of General Literature*, 19, 1828, pp 523-524.

## Selective Family Tree of Gibson Lucas III

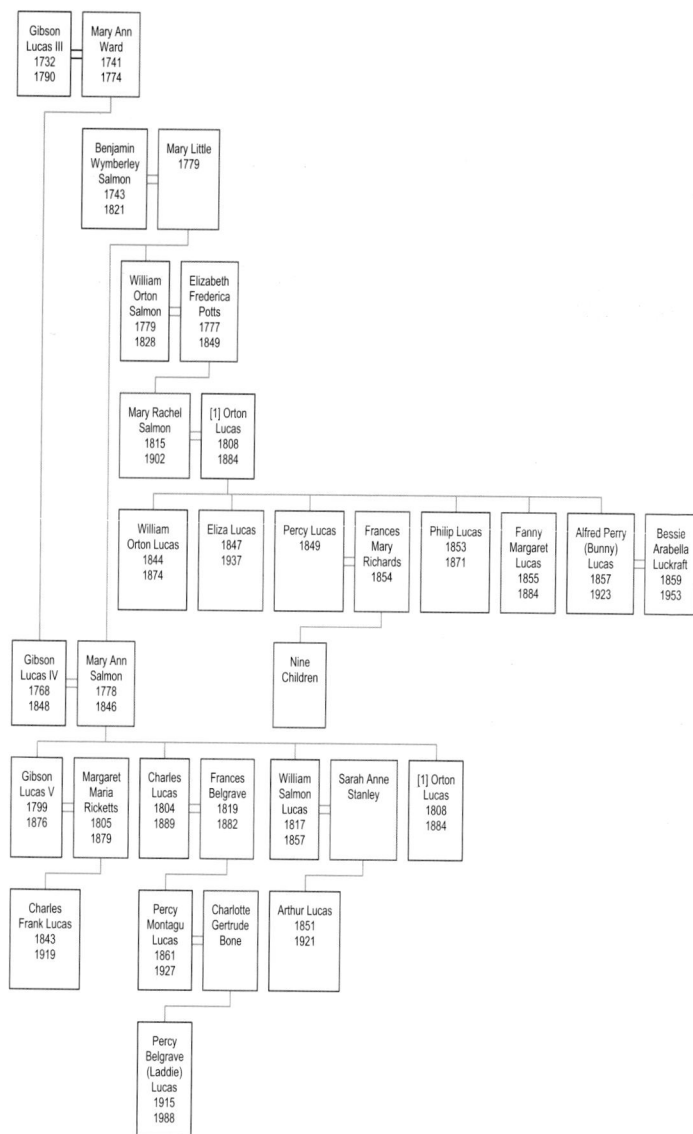

```
Gibson              Mary Ann
Lucas III           Ward
1732                1741
1790                1774

        Benjamin        Mary Little
        Wymberley       1779
        Salmon
        1743
        1821

                William         Elizabeth
                Orton           Frederica
                Salmon          Potts
                1779            1777
                1828            1849

                        Mary Rachel     [1] Orton
                        Salmon          Lucas
                        1815            1808
                        1902            1884

                William     Eliza Lucas   Percy Lucas   Frances   Philip Lucas   Fanny      Alfred Perry   Bessie
                Orton Lucas  1847         1849          Mary       1853          Margaret   (Bunny)        Arabella
                1844                                    Richards                 Lucas      Lucas          Luckraft
                1874                                    1854                     1855       1857           1859
                                                                                1884       1923           1953

Gibson    Mary Ann                            Nine
Lucas IV  Salmon                              Children
1768      1778
1848      1846

Gibson     Margaret     Charles    Frances     William    Sarah Anne    [1] Orton
Lucas V    Maria        Lucas      Belgrave    Salmon      Stanley       Lucas
1799       Ricketts     1804       1819        Lucas                     1808
1876       1805         1889       1882        1817                      1884
           1879                                1857

Charles              Percy       Charlotte    Arthur Lucas
Frank Lucas          Montagu     Gertrude     1851
1843                 Lucas       Bone         1921
1919                 1861
                     1927

                Percy
                Belgrave
                (Laddie)
                Lucas
                1915
                1988
```

**Percy**, the second eldest brother, was born in 1849. He was at Uppingham from April 1862 to October 1866, but was the only one of the brothers not to play in the cricket eleven. He qualified as a solicitor and in 1876 became a partner in the family firm, which he took over after his father's death. He married Frances Mary Richards in 1878 and they had nine children.

**Philip** was born in 1853 and attended Uppingham from April 1865 to October 1870. He was the only one of the four brothers to play in the Uppingham football fifteen,[11] as well as the cricket eleven, although Bunny did later play soccer, tennis and golf. Philip was drowned at Sonning, near Henley, on 23 March 1871, aged only 18, in an incident which would have profoundly affected Bunny, who was fourteen at the time. A pupil of Messrs Maurice and Royds, surgeons of Reading, Philip went out boating on the Thames with two fellow students. The strength of the current drew his out-rigger boat over a weir, and his friend's canoe capsized as he tried to rescue Philip. 'Mr Lucas could swim but little, and Mr Armstrong gallantly endangered his own life in unavailing attempts to save him.' At the inquest two days later, Philip was described as 'a fine young man' and his father, understandably, was 'greatly distressed.' In June the Royal Humane Society bestowed their bronze medal on George Armstrong for his 'courageous efforts.'[12]

\* \* \* \* \*

William Orton Salmon's widow, Elizabeth, had moved to 22 Chesham Place by 1841, and died in 1849. Orton Lucas and his family seem to have used Chesham Place as a town house and stayed on after she died. They remained there until the mid-1860s, when a sign of changing times was that one of the neighbouring houses was taken over by the Russian Embassy. In the early 1850s they also briefly had a home in Norfolk, Old Hall at Ingham, 'a scattered but pleasant village with several nice houses occupied by the owners', of whom Orton Lucas was one.

By 1855, Orton and Mary Lucas and their family had moved to Loseberry, at Claygate near Esher.[13] Surrey had since Tudor times been attractive to anyone wanting to combine business in London with the pleasures of country life. Claygate is close to the Portsmouth road and in the late eighteenth century the building of Claremont Palace brought rich families

---

11    In Philip's time Uppingham played their own fifteen-a-side version of football, but in 1889 the school adopted the Rugby code.

12    *Liverpool Mercury*, 27 March 1871; *Jackson's Oxford Journal*, 1 April 1871; *Lloyd's Weekly Newspaper*, 18 June 1871. Sourced online at nineteenth-century British Library newspapers, October 2009.

13    Post Office, *Essex, Hertfordshire Kent, Middlesex, Surrey, Sussex directory*, 1855. Information about Claygate and Loseberry from: Malcolm W.H.Peebles, *The Claygate Book*, Blackmore Press, 1983; monographs written in 2007 and 2008 by Howard Mallinson and accessed at May 2009; personal correspondence with Mr Mallinson.

into the newly fashionable village. In 1838 the coming of the railway to Esher reduced journey times to London, and there was a further influx of wealthy people. Presumably it was this that encouraged the Lucases to move from their rather remote Norfolk village. The journey to Esher station would have been no great problem for a wealthy family able to keep a stable and groom.

Loseberry is a large and imposing house which was then set in some fifty acres of its own grounds, and is still an important feature of the Green Belt. The household would not have been able to function without servants. In 1861 there was a nurse, an under-nurse, a cook, a housemaid and a groom. They were all born in Norfolk, which suggests that Orton Lucas took them with him from Ingham, or retained links with the family there. Later censuses show that, although the exact make-up varied, there were usually five or six servants living in the house: a gardener and laundress in the next-door cottage may also have been employed by the Lucases.

*A comfortable life.*
*Loseberry, at Claygate near Esher in Surrey, was the Lucas family home for nearly forty years in Victorian times.*

Orton Lucas died in August 1884, just two months after his daughter Fanny. The family had donated a stained-glass window in Philip's memory to Holy Trinity church at Claygate, and donated another in memory of Fanny and Orton.[14] In his will, Orton left £58,916, equivalent to over £3.5

---

14    Holy Trinity church, Claygate, *List of gravestones to be removed*, published by the church in 1997.

million in 2010 values.[15] He specified that the widowed Mary should continue to occupy Loseberry, and the 1891 census showed her 'living on her own means' there, with Eliza, two nieces and four housemaids. In 1893 Mary agreed that Eliza and Bunny should sell the property, for which they got £6,950 (£420,000 today).[16]

In September 1890 the Venerable Albert Seymour, Archdeacon of Barnstaple, employed Percy to obtain £1,639 (£100,000 today) that was payable to him from a life insurance policy.[17] The following February, Percy admitted to receiving the money and claimed that he would invest it, but made a series of excuses and failed to do so. When the census was taken on 5 April 1891, he had decamped with his family to the Devonshire Hotel in Bournemouth. On 9 June he was adjudged bankrupt because he had absconded with the intention of defrauding his client. On 14 November the Law Society declared him guilty of gross professional misconduct and struck him off; another solicitor struck off on the same day for embezzling £1,000 was sentenced to seven years hard labour, so Percy had almost certainly fled the country or somehow managed to adopt a new identity. To squander his father's professional and financial legacy in a mere six years, he must have been remarkably incompetent and extravagant, unless he was exceptionally unfortunate. Nothing more is known of him.

Bunny played no cricket until late June, so it may well be that much of his time was taken up with trying to sort out the repercussions of his brother's crime. As a devout Anglican, he would surely have been appalled by it, particularly as the victim of the fraud was a senior clergyman, to whom he may well have felt an obligation to make restitution.

Percy's wife Frances moved to Bedford, where her youngest daughter, Dorothy, was born early in 1892, so the unfortunate woman must have been pregnant while all this was going on. The 1901 census shows that she was still in Bedford, said to be a widow and 'living on own means'. Most of the children were at private boarding schools, so it seems likely that Bunny and his mother and sister provided for them and Frances, and spent much of their considerable inheritance from Orton Lucas in doing so. His mother died in 1902, aged 86, and left only £1,518, which may be a reflection of the scandal over Percy. Bunny himself had no children so his will, made out in 1904, directed that, after his widow had died, his nine nieces and nephews should inherit the trust fund he set up for her.

---

15    All price comparisons from the currency converter at
       www.nationalarchives.gov.uk/currency
16    National Archive CRES 38/2009.
17    *The Times*, 16 November 1891.

# Chapter Two

## Uppingham School, 1870-1874

In August 1869, A.P.Lucas followed his brothers to Uppingham School. Founded in 1584, it had been a small, high-quality local grammar school, but this was the period when the railways were radically changing many aspects of society. In 1853 Edward Thring was appointed headmaster and Uppingham was transformed into a public school, though not in the very front rank. It was not one of the nine great schools referred to by the Clarendon Commission of 1861-64 as 'significant ... in the public eye', nor in cricket terms were its games played at Lord's or covered in any detail by *Wisden*. It was, though, one of a group known as 'Elevated Grammar Schools' that also included Tonbridge and Repton.[18]

The embodiment of the cult of 'muscular Christianity', Thring developed the idea of an education for the full man, in which team games, classical learning and Anglicanism prepared his boys for their role in governing an empire. Donald P.Leinster-Mackay claimed in the *Dictionary of National Biography* that Thring was 'the greatest public school headmaster during the second half of the nineteenth century.' Canon Hardwicke Rawnsley, co-founder of the National Trust and a contemporary of Philip and Arthur Lucas in the 1870 Uppingham cricket eleven, wrote that Thring was 'the very pulse of the machine'.[19]

*Sixty Years of Uppingham Cricket* is a remarkable book, written by one of H.H.Stephenson's pupils, William Seeds Patterson, who went to great trouble to seek out original sources for his work.[20] He was himself no mean cricketer and played in 41 first-class matches between 1874 and 1882, including three appearances for the Gentlemen in 1876 and 1877. His book gives an inside view of the 'effortlessly superior' schooling enjoyed by upper-middle class Victorian Englishmen. Their fathers' money bought them facilities in the classroom and on the playing field that working class children could scarcely imagine. Between 1853 and 1872 £81,196 was invested in sporting facilities at Uppingham, where the playing fields, said even now to be the largest in the country, 'were themselves significant symbols of security and élitism'.[21] The book is all the more impressive because of its unquestioning assumption that such privileges were right and natural. Servants, shopkeepers, cricket coaches and others of the

---

18    See Mangan, *op cit.*, p 2.
19    In *Edward Thring, Teacher and Poet*, details quoted in Mangan, *op cit.*, p 79.
20    Much of this section is based on Patterson's book, published by Longmans in 1909.
21    See Mangan, *op cit.*, p 100.

lower orders pass like extras across Patterson's stage, seldom referred to as 'Mr' or given a Christian name, unless perhaps they were 'men of a higher class'. His account of Thring's last days is extraordinarily powerful, if slightly bonkers: after suffering a stroke in the school chapel, the headmaster walked slowly 'down the aisle between the kneeling rows of his boys, and passed bravely and silently to his death'.

Patterson's book is dedicated 'to Charles Ernest Green, the "father" of Uppingham cricket, to whose wise generosity and sound judgment are mainly due whatever cricketing fame the school has attained'. Though Green was a fine schoolboy cricketer, his most lasting contribution to Uppingham cricket was not made on the field. After his departure, cricket at the school declined and the batting, in particular, was 'decidedly below what might have been expected from a school of our standing'. By then it had become customary for the public schools to have professional cricketers to coach the boys, but Uppingham employed them only in alternate years. Green, 'with characteristic enthusiasm, and with his charming powers of persuasion, set himself to remove what he saw were the hindrances' to ... winning a reputation in the cricket world. He saw coaching as the key, and was looking for a man who understood the game and possessed 'the high character which would have weight with the boys'. The coach would teach them cricket 'by living among them permanently and establishing a correct and sound style which would percolate throughout the school.'

Green was greatly impressed by Stephenson, first when playing against him and then when Uppingham visited Rossall, the Lancashire school where he was coach. He had in 1859 gone on the first overseas tour – George Parr's to North America – and in 1861/62 had led the first English team to tour Australia. As batsman, bowler and wicket-keeper he 'was a good authority on the game, and had for half his life been in the front rank of cricketers. He came of good stock – his father was a doctor – and he had good manners, a high sense of honour and a generous heart.' The 1861 census listed Stephenson as a professional cricketer, but in 1871 he was shown as a huntsman: even though he went on to play a full season for Surrey, he evidently felt some uncertainty about his position. Shortly after witnessing an inept batting performance by his old school, Green learnt that Stephenson, near the end of his playing career, was looking for 'a more secure employment and home'. Employed in the winter as a huntsman by the exiled Orleanist French royal family, he planned to use his cricket and hunting reputations to set up in business in London.

Green invited Stephenson to settle at Uppingham for the start of the 1872 season and made a generous offer to pay his salary for an experimental first year, but it took all of Green's persuasive powers for him to change his plans. The headmaster, too, had reservations, confiding to his diary on 28 May 1872: 'I do not want cricket to get too powerful in the school here, and to be worshipped and to be made the end of life for a considerable section of the school.' Ironically, he was worried that the coaching was proving too successful: Uppingham thrashed Haileybury by an innings and 250 runs, and he was concerned that 'they are a very nice set of fellows, and it will so spoil their outing'. Within six months the headmaster declared himself satisfied with the arrangements, and had 'a constantly increasing confidence in, and regard for, the school professional.' Evidently he was satisfied that Stephenson's contribution at the school extended beyond cricket. Shortly before his death fifteen years later, Thring wrote: 'Mark me, cricket is the greatest bond of the English-speaking race, and no mere game.'

*H.H.Stephenson.*
*Lucas 'never tired of sayng*
*how much he owed to his*
*teacher'.*

Patterson describes A.P.Lucas's arrival in 1870 'in the First [Eleven] of the Middle ground', a very fine ground above the town that was allotted to boys in the lower school. Lucas was 'then a little round figure of thirteen' who had been 'coached ... by his father and brother on the paternal lawn near Esher'. In the following year he 'remained in the First of the Middle ground [rather than progress to the School first eleven], doubtless owing to his size and age'.

Lucas was in the house of Walter Earle, the joint-founder and first secretary of the Uppingham Rovers, who doubtless encouraged his cricket, but the crucial factor in his development was Stephenson's appointment in 1872. Lucas had made good runs in matches at home during the midsummer holidays, and immediately on his return was selected for the first eleven against the Old Boys. He opened the batting and in the first innings was run out for seven, but in the second made 66 'by excellent play and occasionally showing some fine hitting'. It was said that his 'style of batting shows wonderful promise'. Patterson recalled: 'In this match he fully justified the selection, and the embryo qualities were shown which distinguished his batting for thirty years – the straight bat, and the firm, hard play.' The Red *Lillywhite* annual reviewed the 1872 season: 'Cricket is in a flourishing state at Uppingham, where H.H.Stephenson has taken up his quarters, and is teaching the boys some of that straight play for which he is famous.'

Lucas's cricket continued to improve during 1873, with several fifties and 89 of an opening partnership of 161 against Repton. MCC recognised Uppingham's improvement by sending a team to the school for the first time, and Lucas made 42 and 17 not out in Uppingham's nine-wicket win. Most unusually, a return was arranged, at The Oval, but this time the school lost by nine wickets and only Lucas, who 'carried his bat for about 20' in the first innings and added another 20 in the second, sustained his reputation. He ended the season with 483 runs at 43.91.

In 1874 Patterson and others moved on to university but 'Lucas remained, and was a tower of strength throughout the season'. Now 17, Lucas scored his first century, against Stamford School, and an 81 against G.H.Longman's XI, a strong side brought down by the Cambridge captain which included several Blues. He then played against an MCC team led by C.E.Green, who recalled: 'I chose the team myself and, as I did not want to beat the boys very badly indeed, I took care not to make it too strong. When we had succeeded in getting one wicket down for about 200 ... we thought we had got over our difficulties.'[22] Lucas made 136 in an opening partnership of 271 with T.R.Fleming. In a very disappointing performance against the Old Boys, the school was twice bowled out for 77, but Lucas made 22 which 'showed brilliant cricket until he was run out attempting a third run', and 28. He also took three wickets, including his cousin Arthur for a duck. *Lillywhite* summarised his last season at Uppingham: 'A thorough cricketer all-round, having strong defence and can hit well to any part of the field; a fair wicket-keeper and good change bowler, being slow with a high delivery; a splendid field anywhere.' His season's batting average of 50.33 in twelve completed innings was not surpassed until 1893.

*Lucas (left) with W.S.Patterson, author of 'Sixty Years of Uppingham Cricket'.*

---

22    *Chats on the Cricket Field*, in *The Cricket Field* magazine, 14 October 1893.

Patterson recalled Stephenson's coaching methods. He would bowl 'decidedly above medium but not fast' so as not to frighten the boys 'yet fast enough to keep them active in watching the pitch and defending their wicket.' Mostly he bowled on off and middle stump but he taught them that anything on leg stump should be played firmly off the legs, not in the air but 'along the ground somewhere between square leg and mid on.' Stephenson's teaching was so successful that it became known as the 'Uppingham stroke'.

The great features of Uppingham cricket were thus 'the forward play and the straight bat'. Lucas was not a tall man, so Stephenson's methods were particularly important in the development of his technique:

> It is true that Lucas also showed a great deal of back play, but it must be remembered that Lucas had not as long a reach as some of the others and moreover his back play was as strong and as run-getting as many others' forward play. As a matter of fact, Lucas played both back and forward well, but it is clear that without Stephenson's teaching he would have been only a back player.

Lucas occasionally returned to play against his old school. In 1880 he brought down his own team and contributed a good share to its win by seven wickets, as well as being an excellent host. For the Old Boys he made 95 in 1878, 56 in 1886 and 34 in 1888, while in 1892 he scored 38 and took four wickets. And as late as 1907, aged 50, he turned out for I Zingari, one of the best amateur wandering sides, against the school.

\* \* \* \* \*

Another Old Uppinghamian, Ernest William Hornung, loved cricket but seldom played because of severe asthma. When he sought to emulate the literary success of his brother-in-law Arthur Conan Doyle, he created Raffles, a character whose fame in turn-of-the-century crime fiction is second only to that of Sherlock Holmes. A.J.Raffles attended a public school clearly modelled on Uppingham and was 'the finest slow bowler in England', but was also 'the amateur cracksman'. The nickname of his Watson, 'Bunny' Manders, may well have been a sly tribute to Lucas, who was at the height of his cricketing fame when Hornung was at Uppingham.

George Orwell argued that 'In making Raffles a cricketer as well as a burglar, Hornung was not merely providing him with a plausible disguise; he was also drawing the sharpest moral contrast that he was able to imagine.'[23] Though not referring specifically to Lucas, his comments on style have echoes of Galsworthy's:

---

23    George Orwell, *Raffles and Miss Blandish*, in *Horizon* magazine, October 1944.

> Cricket ... gives expression to a well-marked trait in the English character, the tendency to value 'form' or 'style' more highly than success. In the eyes of any true cricket-lover it is possible for an innings of ten runs to be 'better' (*i.e.* more elegant) than an innings of a hundred runs ... .

Despite constant newspaper reports of his stylish batting, Lucas had a career first-class average of only 26.38, and perhaps exemplified Orwell's comment.

Hornung killed off his anti-hero in the Boer War but later experienced a real-life war tragedy. He wrote *Lord's Leave 1915*, a poem in similar vein to Henry Newbolt's *Vitaï Lampada*[24]:

> No Lord's this year: no silken lawns on which
> A dignified and dainty throng meanders
> The Schools take guard upon a fierier pitch
> Somewhere in Flanders ...

His only son Oscar, captain of games at Eton, compared life in the trenches to 'putting your left leg to the ball at cricket'. He wrote to his uncle, Conan Doyle, declaring: 'It is the one good thing the war has done – to give public school fellows a chance – they are the one class who are enjoying themselves in this war.' On 6 July 1915, Oscar Hornung, a second lieutenant in the Essex Regiment, was killed leading his platoon at Ypres in Flanders.[25]

The Great War had a devastating effect on Uppingham, where no fewer than 447 names appear on the Roll of Honour. They include Edward Brittain, Roland Leighton and Victor Richardson, respectively brother, fiancé and friend of Vera Brittain, who wrote so movingly about their deaths in *Testament of Youth*. Lucas was far too old to serve, but when he revisited his old school he must have played against some of the young men who were later killed, so would have been deeply affected by the losses.

---

24    See Mangan, *op cit.*, p 193.
25    See Birley, *op cit.*, p 206.

## Chapter Three
## Uppingham Rovers, 1874-1913

Lucas also kept up his connection with the school through the Uppingham Rovers Cricket Club, a travelling team of past and present pupils. Among the club's founders were his brother William and C.E.Green, whose friend Edward Rutter suspected was the 'good financial angel' of their tours.[26] Their motto was *Solvitur ambulando*, which can be translated as 'you solve your problems while walking' or, as one of the team had it, as 'life is made better by roving'. They aimed 'to keep up a good standard of cricket, to foster esprit de corps and to form a firm tie between past and present'. Their first-ever match was a close and exciting draw against Rugby School which W.S.Patterson thought 'typical of the Rover spirit – keen to win if it can be done, but if defeat comes, chivalrous enough to accept it cheerfully'. They had no home ground but toured the country playing mostly two-day, two-innings matches. For a while the Rovers were the best of all such travelling amateur teams and from 1879 to 1882 did not have to exercise their cheerful chivalry, because they were not defeated. The team 'could have held its own with any county eleven in the country, and the Central Press Association sent a reporter round with our team to report daily our scores and doings.'[27]

The main source about them is *The Doings of the Uppingham Rovers*, a series of seven large, lovingly compiled, leather-bound books, accurately described by Patterson as 'elephantine volumes'.[28] They are a thoroughly good read and the way in which they are written epitomises the spirit of the Rovers. They record the cricketing and social activities of a group of young men who clearly enjoyed one another's company. Like all such groups, they could be somewhat exclusive and they were sometimes rather condescending towards those less privileged than themselves, but they come over as essentially likeable. Their often juvenile humour was most obviously expressed in excruciatingly bad puns which, in case the reader missed them, were emphasised in italics. Even as a young man, Lucas was rather more serious-minded than some of the others, but he entered into the spirit of their activities and clearly thoroughly enjoyed them. The anecdotes about him are of no great significance, but I have quoted most of them because they give some insight into his character.

26    Edward Rutter, *Cricket Memories*, Williams and Norgate, 1925, p 70.
27    C.E.Green to the Rovers' 'Jubilee' dinner, 1913.
28    I am very grateful to David Ashworth, president of the Uppingham Rovers, who kindly allowed me to see *The Doings* and made me most welcome. David broke Bunny's record for the highest aggregate of runs scored for the Rovers although, as he was careful to point out, it took him about 25 more innings.

*'Elephantine volumes': 'The Doings of the Uppingham Rovers'.*

Lucas was elected as a member of the Rovers and made his debut for them in July 1874, while still at the school. For the Rovers' annual dinner, The Rhyming Rover regularly set words to a familiar tune, producing clever and witty doggerel that scanned almost as badly as that of William McGonagall, who flourished around the same time. He recorded Lucas's contribution to an innings win over Prince's Club and Ground side, at Chelsea:

> That young Lucas must have found it far from easy work to run
> Over turf like asphalt pavement underneath a broiling sun
> What a first-rate bat he is, though. Draper looked in quite a fix
> When against his straightest bowling Lucas knocked up seventy-six ...

In 1875 Lucas and Patterson were elected as the Cambridge University representatives on the Rovers' committee. In his account of a match against Crystal Palace, the chronicler gave an insight into the characters of the two young men:

> As Patterson was supposed to be troubled with 'nerves' and senses while Lucas was reported to be devoid of such encumbrances, they were put in first together ... . The fellow Cantabs hit about in excellent style until Lucas (while laughing at a joke he had heard the night before, and which he had just discerned the point of) made a mistake and was bowled ... .

Against Tooting, the pair added an extraordinary unbroken partnership of 238 in two hours, Lucas 130 and Patterson 93. Due in next was a joint-founder of the Rovers, Jack Beevor, who complained that he 'had not come all the way from Nottingham to see these two youngsters bat.' Aged only 18, Lucas headed the Rovers' averages with 264 runs at 52.80.

In 1876 the Rovers embarked, for the first time, on 'an autumn campaign in the north'. Lucas had a fine match against the Gentlemen of Staffordshire, with exactly 100 and eight wickets, including four caught-and-bowled. He 'completely crumpled up the Staffordshire bowling' and 'also did much execution in the bowling department and brought off some wonderful catches'. It was in this season that his bowling, which had previously been described as 'mere treacle', first came into its own.

*The Uppingham Rovers in 1876,*
*with Lucas on the right of the middle row holding a bat.*

The Rovers delighted in giving one another nicknames, and part of the fun was making them as obscure as possible: Charles Ernest Ridley, for example, was 'Bob', and Francis Barry Whitfeld 'Billy.' When Lucas first played for them he was mysteriously called 'the Shah' or the 'Persian Gun', later modified to 'The Little Gun', to complement C.E.Green who was 'The Big Gun.' It was almost certainly they who gave Lucas the nickname 'Bunny', which was first recorded in *The Same Old Game*, perhaps the best-known of The Rhyming Rover's efforts. It was written for the annual dinner on 6 July 1877, after five of the Rovers were in the Cambridge team unexpectedly defeated by Oxford:

> Our gallant Cambridge Blues,
> Though they didn't win but lose,
> We've proved them and we know what they can do,
> For *Steel's* a man of *mettle*
> And Bunny's in fine fettle,
> And Patterson's a bowler good and true ...

*Chorus*
The same old game,
The same old game,
To forget it or forgo it were a shame.
When we are past and gone,
The young ones coming on,
Will carry on the same old game.

*An Intercepted Letter from a Lady Rover* was an amusing spoof letter from 'Florence' to a female friend, recorded in *The Doings* in 1881. In it, 'Florence' could get no more sensible explanation than that Bunny referred to 'the "rare-bit" of batting Lucas always shows when he goes to the wicket.' The early Rovers deliberately kept the reasons for their nicknames a secret at the time, and now they are long 'past and gone' we are unlikely ever to know why Lucas became Bunny.

The 1877 northern tour was 'the most successful tour ever', and Lucas, now aged 20, played an important part. In an innings win against Birkenhead Park, he scored 58 and took six wickets, and against Castleton he 'made them bite' for seven wickets. After he was caught in heavy rain at York 'a Turkish bath was nearly the end of poor Bunny', but 57 against the Gentlemen of Yorkshire showed that he had recovered from any ill-effects.

Another match in 1877 possibly sowed the seeds for one of the most significant changes, not only in Lucas's cricket career but in his entire life – his move to the county of Essex. For him, as for all the Rovers, the social aspects of the tours were at least as important as the cricket, and their chronicler was unusually effusive about the new Essex club, which had been formed the previous year:

> In former times when our vagrant band went east from Shoreditch it was to Navestock Common that they wended their way. But things have changed since those days. The county has banded together and set up its cricketing tabernacle on a capital piece of turf at Brentwood, and thither the Rovers proceeded to encounter the might and chivalry of the whole shire. Rumour had been heavy with pleasant tales of the new club and its matches, and rumour was no deceiver in this instance, for the reality quite came up to the fondest expectation. Pleasant company, and plenty of it; charming toilets; music, tea, talk, tennis; general hospitality and the heartiest of welcomes. What more could a Rover ask for?

He could perhaps have asked for a decent game of cricket, and he got that too. Essex recovered from a poor start to draw the twelve-a-side match, Lucas taking 12 wickets with his 'loblollies'. C.E.Green, who was born in Essex, later became chairman of the club and persuaded Lucas to qualify for them by residence; it may be that their shared memories of this and other matches against Essex helped Green encourage Lucas to make his life-changing decision. Essex and the other non-first-class county sides the Rovers played in this period were mostly made up of good amateur players, some of whom had played first-class cricket for other counties, MCC or the universities. Rovers' sides usually had a majority with first-class experience, so the cricket was generally of a high standard.

The scorecard of this match, played at the Brentwood County Ground on 3 and 4 August 1877, and Bunny's first recorded game in Essex, is set out below, although unfortunately the full bowling details have now been lost. Ten of the twenty-four players appeared in first-class cricket in their time, so like many other Rovers' matches it was of no mean standard.

**Gentlemen of Essex**

| | | | | |
|---|---|---|---|---|
| C.H.S.Escott | c and b Gibson | 12 | b A.P.Lucas | 7 |
| H.B.Rowan | c C.C.Ridley b A.P.Lucas | 21 | c A.Lucas b A.P.Lucas | 32 |
| C.Sewell | c Green b A.P.Lucas | 5 | c Shadwell b Perkins | 58 |
| W.H.Fowler | c and b Gibson | 14 | st C.C.Ridley b Gibson | 7 |
| G.B.Meares | b Gibson | 0 | b A.P.Lucas | 4 |
| H.Fowler | c A.P.Lucas b Gibson | 12 | b Shadwell | 55 |
| R.Pryor | c Gibson b A.P.Lucas | 3 | not out | 41 |
| J.Round | b A.P.Lucas | 2 | b Shadwell | 5 |
| F.Heatley | c Green b A.P.Lucas | 0 | b Shadwell | 2 |
| W.Pearce | c Green b A.P.Lucas | 6 | st C.C.Ridley b A.P.Lucas | 39 |
| F.Green | c and b A.P.Lucas | 2 | c A.P.Lucas b Shadwell | 1 |
| F.McMullen | not out | 5 | c and b A.P.Lucas | 0 |
| Extras | b 2 | 2 | b 16, w 1 | 17 |
| Totals | | 84 | | 268 |

**Uppingham Rovers**

| | | | | |
|---|---|---|---|---|
| A.P.Lucas | c and b Escott | 38 | c Meares b Escott | 0 |
| C.C.Ridley | c Round b Escott | 0 | c Sewell b Escott | 4 |
| J.Perkins | c and b Meares | 3 | | |
| F.E.Street | b W.H.Fowler | 24 | not out | 30 |
| C.E.Green | b Meares | 29 | not out | 24 |
| H.Gibson | c Meares b W.H.Fowler | 0 | | |
| T.Bell | c Escott b W.H.Fowler | 8 | | |
| G.Borthwick | c Escott b W.H.Fowler | 15 | | |
| F.B.Shadwell | b W.H.Fowler | 1 | | |
| A.Lucas | b Pearce | 3 | | |
| W.de Zoete | run out | 17 | | |
| C.E.Ridley | not out | 0 | [not given] | 17 |
| Extras | b 8, lb 1, nb 1 | 10 | b 1, lb 1, nb 1 | 3 |
| Totals | | 148 | (for three wickets) | 78 |

Result: Match drawn

In July 1878 illness kept Lucas out of the Cambridge University team that famously thrashed the Australians, but by 12 August at Northampton he was sufficiently recovered to 'cart Messrs Pater & Co about in fine form' for 119 out of 230: 'We doubt if Lucas ever played a finer innings; it was a fitting performance to signalize [display in a striking manner] his return to the cricket-field; and did more, we are sure, to complete his recovery than another month by the sad sea waves would have done.'

It was the year of Disraeli's confrontation with Russia over her threatened invasion of Turkey, and The Rhyming Rover came up with his own take on the music hall hit of the day:

> Yes we must have it right and by Jingo when we do,
> We've got the bats, we've got the fields, we've got the bowlers too ...
> ... Of the Surrey team we take the cream, I mean of course young Bunny,
> Of all the bats in England he's the man for my money ...

Against Leeds Clarence, Lucas's dismissal was described as 'thrown out by Scott', which perhaps meant run out by a direct hit. Even more unusual was the case of Francis Hogg who, after the Rovers had beaten Richmond, was recorded as 'went home for tea ... 0'. The chronicler summarised the Rovers' feelings when the tour ended:

> After a fortnight's tour with such good fellows as the Rovers, it is indeed chokey work to say adieu. We took our several ways back to the lonely hearth or the dingy office, sadly and reluctantly, but with a confident hope that we shall have many more meetings as pleasant as that which has just concluded.

Lucas ended the season fourth on the all-time list of Rovers batsmen with 1,339 runs, and fifth among the bowlers with 81 wickets.

In 1879 the tour again began at Northampton, where the atmosphere was decidedly different from that at Essex. On a fast wicket Northamptonshire made 285, accompanied by 'loud expressions of the great unwashed outside the boarding with which, to Charlie Green's great disgust, the ground had been enclosed.' Undaunted, Lucas, no longer at Cambridge, 'was very confident and said "I can always make a hundred here" – and he did too.' In the next game, 'we doubt if Lucas ever played a better innings than his 50 for us, while his eight wickets in the Leicestershire second innings were the result of first-class bowling.' His figures of eight for 38 were to remain the best of his career at any level.

Against the Gentlemen of Sussex at Hove, 'Lucas was (for him) very free' in scoring 89 out of 197 and then 'magnanimously bowled against the wind', which was reported as very strong. He took eight for 28 in the match as a whole. He bowled unchanged throughout both innings of the opposition, as did the much faster Hugh Rotherham, who took full advantage of the wind with eleven for 32. It heralded heavy rain which washed out the next game, at Eastbourne against Devonshire Park, so 'there was nothing to do but rink [skate]. ... A small boy, who rejoiced in the name of "Boss", was seized with an intense admiration for Bunny Lucas, and never left his side, which was fortunate for Bunny as he was thus saved from many a fall.'

In 1880 the newly elected Liberal government brought forward a Ground Game Bill, authorising farmers to kill game on their own farms, and so relieving them from the obligation of feeding their landlords' animals. Ground game was defined as 'animals that live on the ground, such as hares and rabbits', and the issue was of some importance to the landowning classes that were well represented among the Rovers, so The Rhyming Rover had his own take on it:

> We've heard a deal of talk of late about a Ground Game Bill,
> What matter does it make to us we've our Hare and 'Rabbit' still
> And spite of legislation and all that sort of stuff
> On Monday next at Lord's our Bunny will give the Players snuff...

*An affectionate - even sentimental - tribute to the Rovers' star player.*
*The photograph was taken on the Australian tour of 1878/79.*

The Rovers' 'hare' was John Hugh Montague Hare of Docking Hall in Norfolk, but their 'rabbit' failed to 'give the Players snuff', being bowled for nought and two.

Lucas had been badly out of form in first-class cricket but came back to his best with a Rovers side that enjoyed a fine season. Their first fixture, against Essex, was also a popular social event and 'Bunny performed in rare style at the ball'. On the field he scored 22 opening with Green, and took eight wickets in an innings win.

Lucas had scored centuries in the two previous games at Northampton, so the chronicler recorded that 'the Northampton match is Bunny's annual benefit and, in fact, so confident was he of making a century that he magnanimously offered to forgo his innings if they would credit him with

101.' In the event, he made 119 out of 229 and then 'found the spot' with six wickets in the match. In the next game he made only four but took six for 11 as he and Rotherham dismissed Leicestershire for 25, and in the second innings he took five more wickets. Against the Gentlemen of Lancashire at Old Trafford, 'Bunny, not having made a century for two whole days, made a century and a half, which was better'. He again bowled unchanged in the first innings with Rotherham, though this time he took only two wickets. The Rovers had won the first three games of their northern tour by an innings.

Such was Lucas's reputation that when Firth, the Wakefield groundsman, bowled him for seven, Firth 'tossed his cap in the air' and 'his delight was something to behold'. Against Castleton, Lucas was first given out caught at the wicket off his pad and then – when he was the Rovers' only hope of winning a rain-affected game – run out by his partner, but there is no record that he protested at these misfortunes.

The Rovers moved on to a short tour of Sussex. Lucas made 85 and took six wickets in an innings win against East Sussex at Lewes, and then 'we had heard such disquieting rumours of the Devonshire Park lot that Bunny and Rotherham were sent to bed at 7pm on Tuesday night'. Evidently the curfew was effective, for Lucas made 97 and took four wickets, and Rotherham took 14 in another innings win. In the final game of the Rovers' season, 'Bunny got himself out for 103' against Horsham, but the match was drawn. In ten matches Lucas scored 671 runs at 55.91, and played himself back into the form that enabled him, in early September, to share with W.G.Grace the first-ever century partnership in Test cricket.

The 1881 season was even better for the Rovers and for their star player. Against the Gentlemen of Bedfordshire, 'Bunny amused himself all afternoon with bat and ball', scoring 86 and taking ten wickets with 'first-class bowling' in an innings win. Against the Gentlemen of Derbyshire he scored 203 – the only double century of his career: 'Bunny played grand cricket until he had reached 140, then gave the field practice in catching – and they needed it.' Against a team styled Gentlemen of Lancashire, but including three professionals to do the bowling, he scored 67 and then took six for 62 in the Lancashire second innings. Johnny Briggs and Alec Watson bowled so tightly that it took the Rovers 106 balls to score the eleven runs needed to win, with Lucas five not out.

Back in Sussex, against Priory Park Chichester, 'Bunny was terribly upset at being bowled [for six] by a youth in a pink coat called Smith' who, as Sir Charles Aubrey Smith, was to become better known than Lucas. At Horsham the Rovers put on their own 'theatricals followed by yeomanry in which the audience joined ... Bunny was happy the whole time' and scored 134 in an innings win.

For Lucas, the game against Lewes Priory was perhaps more significant for events off the field, where 'in the evening Mrs Luckraft kindly gave us the opportunity of showing off our steps' at her rather grand Italianate house in Wallands Crescent. Presumably present at the dance was her 21-year-old daughter Bessie, who four years later married Lucas. A year later, 'Florence' wrote in *An Intercepted Letter from a Lady Rover* that 'Mr Lucas is such a good young man, and so sweet tempered. I believe he is in love, for I once saw him scratching a name on the ground with the point of a stump – you see I know all the proper cricket terms.' Certainly among the opposition at the match were the Hon Ivo Bligh, of Ashes fame, and Herbert Whitfeld, who was the brother of another Rover and best man at the wedding. On the field, 'Rain robbed us of another victory but perhaps a wet day was more in harmony with our feelings, for the breaking up of our merry band was a trial to us all.'

The chronicler summarised Lucas's outstanding contribution to a memorable season, in which he played all ten matches: 'A.P.Lucas is far ahead in batting. With an average of 66.5 in the three weeks he has made 599 runs ... . In getting all those runs he displayed all his well-known patience, his defence was superb and he punished any loose bowling with great vigour.' He also took 35 wickets for 419 runs, an average of 11.97.

In 1882 The Rhyming Rover took his inspiration from *The Captain's Song* in *H.M.S Pinafore*:

> If you look down the list of Rovers I wist
> Many good bats you will find
> First of all the famous Bunny is the man for our money
> The best bat in England to my mind ...

> ... Of bowlers fast and slow we have plenty to show
> And jolly good bowlers too
> There's Herbert and there's Sandy and Bunny too is handy
> With the style called 'Cock-a-doodle-do.'

The Rovers' chronicler in 1881, and perhaps earlier, was 'H.G.' (Henry Gibson). He did not play for them in 1882, and *The Doings* only have brief factual reports of that season's matches. At the start of their tour Lucas was 'rather out of form', but against Bedfordshire he made 51 not out and had match figures of eight for 65. Against his future county he 'hit well for 65', and Essex lost by an innings.

In 1883 the normal style of reporting was resumed by Gibson or someone else writing in a similar vein, and a 'poet' rather less talented than The Rhyming Rover. Inspired by Lucas's remarkable record against Northamptonshire, he wrote:

> He gets a century a year, he'll do it again I fear,
> Be it medium fast or slow, he gives them all the go, and makes the fields all blow ...

But this time the Rovers found a sticky wicket rather than the usual fast and true one: Lucas could manage only 17 out of 43 all out, and the Rovers had the worst of a draw. Against Lancashire at Old Trafford he was 'up to his old games again ... being ultimately secured in his anxiety to give them the long handle, [he was out for 102] having played perfect cricket for his century.' Against Derbyshire Lucas 'played a steady game with 17 singles in 23, a striking – that is not the word – contrast with his captain.' Green made 65 and, during the lunch interval, demonstrated that he could have qualified as a member of the Drones Club by making an assegai out of a three-foot bread roll, a fork, a napkin and some chutney. He then threw it at Lucas who 'did not seem to *relish* the experience.'

Bad luck with weather and injuries led to a disappointing 1883 season in which the Rovers had only one win, one defeat and no fewer than seven draws. At Huddersfield, Lucas made 78 and at Bradford he 'batted as perfectly as ever, securing another century. He finished with a fine square leg hit for six out of the ground.' Against the Gentlemen of Yorkshire, he made 120 and did the hat-trick. At Portsmouth, 'the Hampshire umpire had no doubt been reading about his centuries in the paper and gave him out lbw almost before he was appealed to.' Stephenson, who toured with the Rovers as their umpire, by contrast refused to give a catch at the wicket claimed by the Rovers and 'made himself awfully disliked.' They blamed that decision, and the absence of Schultz because of his business partner's illness, for their first defeat since 1878. They had been so successful in the previous few years that they perhaps rather lost sight of their cheerful chivalry, and the chronicler was slightly tetchy about their reverses. Lucas nevertheless scored 625 runs at 48.07 and took 32 wickets at 12.59.

In 1884 the Rovers as usual began their northern tour at Northampton, but it cannot have been their favourite venue, even though they won by an innings. They were again barracked by partial spectators, one of whom 'tried to lift their purses'. Lucas made only 28 and 10 but took seven wickets and as they left, 'the small fry crowded round the drag to see "Leeucas" smile.' As a regular for England and the Gentlemen, he was the best-known of the Rovers and a considerable draw for the general public.

The game at Leicester was 'a red-letter day' for the Rovers. Despite 15 and 34 from Lucas, the home side had the best of things and were set only 53 to win. Lucas and Rotherham reduced them to 13 for seven, but Leicestershire gradually crept towards the target until they needed two to win with the last pair together. 'Then amid the wildest excitement Lucas clean bowled Coleman and left us the match by one run.' Lucas had bowled unchanged with Rotherham and finished with five for 26.

Lucas's father died a few days after this game so he was able to play in only two more Rovers matches. Unusually, he had a poor time with the bat – only 100 runs in seven innings – but took 28 wickets at 9.21. The Rovers returned to their best form with seven wins and only one draw and one defeat.

At the end of the season, there was a summary of the Rovers' doings over the previous 21 years. They had won 87 games, drawn 59 and lost 32. They suffered no defeat from 1879 to 1882, and only one in 1883 and one in

1884. The 1875 partnership between Lucas and Patterson remained their most remarkable batting achievement. Green, with 4,391 runs, was the leading run scorer but Lucas, with 4,062, was rapidly catching him up, and his twelve centuries were as many as all the others put together. More surprisingly, his 292 wickets placed him second on the bowling list behind Rotherham with 408. The conclusion was unarguable: 'The Rovers' Club fairly deserves the reputation which it now enjoys of being the strongest wandering club in the kingdom.'

Lucas missed the 1885 season through illness and he came back to cricket on 30 June 1886, playing against the school for an Old Boys' team consisting entirely of Rovers. The chronicler described his return at some length:

> Lucas, who evidently has not forgotten how to play cricket during his illness, showed us some fine cricket in something of his old style. He rather alarmed the Ladies in the pavilion by sending a fine hit into their midst. His innings of 53 contained three fours and seven threes, and throughout he showed good form and hard hitting though, we believe, this is the first time he has played for two seasons.

As with his briefer absence in 1878, he eased himself back into the game with the slightly less demanding cricket of the Rovers.

Essex County Cricket Club was now in its first full season at Leyton and Green, as chairman and captain, committed himself fully to its development. He therefore stood down as captain and secretary of the Rovers in favour of his friend Lucas. *The Doings* record:

> A most successful tour was accomplished under the able generalship of A.P.Lucas. On him fall the honours of the tour. We would congratulate him on his reappearance in the cricket field and hope to see him in his old form with the willow next year.

Against Eastbourne he scored 80 and took six wickets in a ten-wicket win, but he was not quite back at his best with the bat, scoring 230 runs in nine innings, although he did head the bowling with 21 wickets at 15.50.

In the 1887 season, Lucas duly recovered his old form and his place at the top of the batting averages with 389 runs at 43.22, and he also took 12 wickets. Playing against the Manchester club, in effect the Lancashire Second XI, the Rovers came up against Arthur Mold, who fourteen years later was no-balled for throwing and left the game. Some commentators claimed that Mold was ill-used, but Sydney Pardon in *Wisden* argued that he was lucky to get away with it for as long as he did, and the Rovers would certainly have endorsed that view: 'We had never known anyone throw so fast and so straight; in fact, it was suggested that Lucas should give his nickname up, and that he should be nicknamed Bungo.' Lucas was untroubled by Mold and 'played grandly for his 84', but Manchester won by eight wickets.

When the party travelled south, 'Bunny went off to see his wife' and the team started their game against Hampshire Club and Ground. They had passed 500 when the ninth wicket fell and ...

> After a short interval our last man arrived, slowly buttoning his glove. 'Who's your last man?' asked the elated bowler to H.H. 'Is he a setting shot?' 'Well, sometimes he is,' replied H.H., 'but sometimes he keeps up his wicket for quite a considerable time; he's got quite a fair defence; he's A.P. Luc- ' The bowler gave a howl of despair and walked off.

In the event Lucas took pity on his opponents and gave his wicket away for 23, but the Rovers won by an innings.

Against the United Services, 'when Bunny lost the toss, we felt something extraordinary was going to happen' and it did. The home team were bowled out for 191 and then the Rovers piled up 659 for four. Schultz's 286 remains the Rovers' highest individual score, while Lionel Martineau made 184 not out and Lucas a mere 50.

Lucas was re-elected captain in 1888. His century against the United Services ...

> added one more to the masterly displays he has shown during his long and valuable service with the Rovers. A more powerful display of cricket has perhaps seldom been seen, his figures, which included eleven fours, seven threes, eleven twos and 27 singles, speaking for themselves.

He made 114 out of 215 but the game ended in a draw. In the next game, against Eastbourne, 'Lucas continued his fine cricket form of the previous match. His form was as perfect as ever and the spectators gave him a worthy reception on his retirement in return for the treat he had given them.' The summary of the season noted that 'Bunny, the captain, would bowl lobs, with a threatened resignation of the whole team in consequence.' They may well have been right, for he took only three wickets for 103, and also scored 288 runs in ten innings.

On the 1889 tour, Lucas, by now a player with some 150 first-class matches to his credit, had a fine time in Yorkshire. Against the Yorkshire Gentlemen he scored 27 in a low-scoring innings win. At Huddersfield he was 'in magnificent form' with exactly half of the total – 178 out of 356, and the Rovers had the best of a draw. Against Bradford he scored 96 out of 253 but again the Rovers could not quite force the win.

Returning south to Eastbourne, 'Bunny scored at a terrific pace and notched a century' before lunch, finishing with 124 out of 492 in an innings win. The chronicler noted that the new ground at The Saffrons, dedicated to cricket, was far better than the old one at Devonshire Park, which had a variety of public uses. Against the United Services 'Bunny's donkey- drops proved more than useful,' and at Horsham he 'continued his defence well into the second day' for 75 out of 372 in an innings win. In the season as a whole the Rovers won two and drew four, two very favourably:

Our captain must have been delighted with the results, to which he had added no small measure of success. He bats well, tosses well (only losing five out of six of the spins of the coin) and bowls well.

Lucas scored 570 runs in seven innings and took ten wickets at 13.90.

In the first game of the 1890 Yorkshire tour, 'Bunny had the "A.P.Luc-" to win the toss against the Gentlemen of Yorkshire.' It is an indication of the spirit in which Lucas and the Rovers played their cricket that 'Lusty' (J.H.Roberts) took two for 4 but 'looked so frightfully conceited that Bunny soon had him off.' At Harrogate, a man called Hudson turned up without cricket flannels and played in dark trousers, so had to ask Lucas's permission to bowl. Bunny 'was rather obstinate with his ear' and had to be asked several times, but eventually he agreed and Hudson showed his gratitude by bowling him second ball. Whether this was 'selective hearing' or an early manifestation of Lucas's genuine deafness is unclear. When the party was due to move on to play the North and East Riding,

> Bunny, with a view to making sure we were all on time, murmured that our train for Malton went at 'ten to': I looked it out and found he meant 10.02. Had an excellent breakfast and caught the train. Skipper thoroughly enjoyed himself and notched 142 in his best form.

Lucas also took five wickets in an innings win.

On 24 July 1890, in the Rovers match at Portsmouth against the United Services, Lucas dismissed Conan Doyle, whose Sherlock Holmes stories were just becoming bestsellers, in a manner that left the author 'longing to kick oneself for one's foolishness all the way to the pavilion.' Doyle recalled the incident in his 1924 autobiography:[29]

> I was bowled by A.P.Lucas, by the most singular ball that I have ever received. He propelled the ball like a quoit in the air to a height of at least 30 feet, and it fell straight and true on to the top of the bails. I have often wondered what a good batsman would have made of that ball. To play it one would have needed to turn the blade of the bat straight up, and could hardly fail to give a chance. I tried to cut it off my stumps, with the result that I knocked down my wicket and broke my bat, while the ball fell in the midst of this general chaos … .

The incident inspired Doyle to write *The Story of Spedegue's Dropper* - an improbable, but entertaining, short story about an asthmatic schoolteacher who used a series of such deliveries to win The Ashes for England.[30]

---

29    Doyle, A.Conan, *Memories and Adventures,* Oxford University Press [1989 edition], p 283.

30    Curiously, Doyle did not publish the story until 1929, almost forty years later. Perhaps writing his autobiography reminded him of the incident and inspired the story. He had a great affection for the Rovers and wrote a little verse in their honour: 'You Rovers have the name / I have heard it near and far / That you are a merry family / UR, UR, UR.'

Lucas was neither the first nor the last to bowl donkey-drops and, in the late 1950s, the Leicestershire secretary-captain Charles Palmer – partly inspired by his love for *The Story of Spedegue's Dropper* – took a dozen or more first-class wickets with them. He commented to Douglas Miller:

> The success of this type of ball depends on several things. It must be high enough for a steep descent, at least 30 feet, or it will merely be a full toss. It must be straight; it must be full enough length to land on or very near the stumps if missed. And it must be used sparingly enough to be something of a surprise to the batsman.[31]

From 2000 Lucas and Palmer would not have been able to bowl donkey-drops, for they became illegal when the law relating to full tosses was broadened to include those that are not fast.

Lucas headed the 1890 batting averages with 265 at 44.16 and took 13 wickets at 12.61. The chronicler concluded his report with a note that Lucas 'has promised to take us all for three weeks next year and bring H.H.', but evidently circumstances – possibly the scandal over brother Percy's embezzlement – brought about a change of plan. In 1891

> Bunny was unable to be with us this year. … When we have to record the loss of his general self and the consequent loss to the side of his always colossal average it is indeed a sad matter … .

Lucas had been the Rovers' finest player for seventeen years, but his time with them was all but ended. Perhaps because of his career on the Stock Exchange and increasing commitments to Essex, he played only three more games for them.

In 1896 he returned for two matches. At Northampton, 'knowing that he never took less than 100 *v* Northants we felt quite happy. Nor was our confidence misplaced, his 106, except for a difficult chance in the slips, being faultless.' Then he made 68 against the Gentlemen of Derbyshire and 'we lost Bunny here, who was compelled to leave us, much to our mutual sorrow. However, two matches are better than none, and we can only hope that he will be able to come on the whole tour with us next year.'

That hope went unfulfilled, but there was to be one last hurrah. In 1913 the Rovers held a splendid Golden Jubilee dinner at the Hotel Cecil, and Lucas was among the most distinguished of the guests. In a wide-ranging speech summarising the achievements of the Rovers, C.E.Green paid tribute to 'A.P.Lucas, the finest batsman and one of the keenest cricketers that Uppingham has ever produced … who still goes on playing, and making runs, in his own inimitable style.' Doubtless to mark the occasion, Lucas had turned out for the Rovers a few days earlier, at Beckenham against the Old Abbeians. After the Rovers had fielded all day, 'their innings was remarkable for an innings of 65 not out by Bunny, who seems to get

---

31    Douglas Miller, *Charles Palmer: More Than Just a Gentleman,* Fairfield Books, 2005.

younger with declining years.' After his death, the Rovers' secretary, C.S.Hurst, recalled in *The Doings*: 'I personally saw him play only once. It was his last innings for the Rovers – in 1913. The wicket was not good, the bowling was not slow, and the batsman was approaching 60 years of age. He scored 65 very comfortably and then "retired" in order to catch his train to London.'

Chris Hurst's recollection was part of a fine memorial tribute by a talented cricketer of a later generation, who in the early 1900s captained Uppingham and Oxford,[32] and then played for the Gentlemen and Kent:

> A.P.Lucas arrived on the scene when the days of infancy were past. ... So many fine cricketers contributed to the Rovers' achievements over so long a period that any attempt to apportion the credit would be invidious. But I think that every one of them would agree that no one did as much as Bunny Lucas. The soundest and greatest batsman that ever came out of Uppingham, he was also a more than useful bowler, and his record for the Rovers is astonishing. He played regularly from 1874 to 1890 (except 1885). In those tours he played 155 innings, not including any Old Boys' matches and counting six other innings which he played in later years. His total batting figures were 161 innings, ten not outs, 6,060 runs.
>
> As a bowler he took eight wickets in an innings against Leicestershire in 1879, and on nineteen other occasions he took five wickets or more in an innings and his total bag amounted to 371, the third largest in the Rovers' records.
>
> Bearing in mind that Lucas in his time ranked only behind W.G.Grace and A.G.Steel among all-round amateur cricketers, and that his Rovers cricket was played when his powers were at his greatest and when the demands of 'big' cricket were at their highest, it is difficult to imagine that any man could have given greater service to an Old Boys' club.

---

32    Hurst played 47 first-class matches in all, scoring as a middle-order batsman, 1,787 runs at 23.51. He became a senior civil servant, involved for many years with the coal industry.

# Chapter Four

## Surrey and Cambridge University, 1874-1878

H.H.Stephenson retired from first-class cricket in 1871 but ensured that his old county was made aware of the potential of his young protégé, who was qualified for them by residence. While still a pupil at Uppingham, Lucas made his first-class and Surrey debut on 16 July 1874 at The Oval against Middlesex. Aged 17 years and 148 days, he was at that time the youngest person to play for Surrey in first-class cricket. Exactly as he had in his first game for the Uppingham first eleven, he opened the innings and was run out for seven, perhaps underestimating his opponents' skills at a higher level of the game. In the second innings he was bowled for 20.

On 20 July at Prince's, where he had scored 76 for the Rovers a few days earlier, Lucas was selected for the Gentlemen of the South against the Players of the North. The Players won the toss and batted. While W.G.Grace steadily picked up five wickets at one end, including two catches held by Lucas, his brother Fred was unsuccessful at the other. Lucas came on as first and only change bowler. He soon had the Players' top scorer, William Oscroft, stumped and Arnold Rylott caught, finishing with two for 41. The Players were all out for 147 and by close of play the Gentlemen were 209 for six, with Lucas not out 48. Rylott caught and bowled him before he added to that score and the Players fought back: by the end of the second day the Gentlemen were 57 for four needing a further 67 to win. On the third morning Lucas and Fred Grace put together a partnership of 56 before Lucas was bowled by Shaw, but the Gentlemen won by four wickets.

Half a century later, *The Times* in Lucas's obituary commented:

> As regards the early development of his powers he belonged to a very select band. Mr. Lucas did not appear for Gentlemen *v* Players as a schoolboy, but he came very near it. In 1874 – the year he left Uppingham – he was picked for the Gentlemen of the South against the Players of the North at Prince's, and scored 48 and 23. His form in those two innings – against Alfred Shaw and Morley at their best – left no doubt as to his class. It was felt by all good judges that a new star had been discovered. ... When he jumped into fame at Prince's, Mr. Lucas was under seventeen and a half ... he never looked back.

Lord Harris recalled it was said that when Lucas was batting against Shaw and Morley 'the bowler only needed a mid-on and mid-off, as he played so straight back; but, mark you, hard enough to go to the boundary generally – there was no letting the ball hit the bat with him.'[33] Despite this success he played only one more first-class game in 1874, scoring 12 in Surrey's innings win over Sussex. He may well have had to return to school; and also, his brother William was seriously ill and died on 23 September.

Rather unusually, Lucas went up to Clare College three weeks before his 18th birthday in the Lent term, the second of the academic year – some eight months earlier than might have been expected. If there was some special reason for these arrangements, I have not traced it. Unlike his brother William and his cousin Arthur, he did not win an exhibition to university, so perhaps was not quite as academically gifted as them.

Clare, the second oldest of Cambridge's thirty-one colleges, was founded in 1326, and generously endowed a few years later by Lady Elizabeth de Clare, a granddaughter of King Edward I.[34] The college steadily grew in size and wealth so in the seventeenth century the college erected the present majestic buildings, which were matched by the college's achievements. The college also bought a field on the other side of the Cam and built the famous Clare Bridge, now the oldest across the river. The field became the college cricket ground and, despite their small numbers, the team achieved some success to which Lucas may well have contributed, although no records survive. In the 1930s the new University Library building was erected on the site.

By the time Lucas arrived, Clare had declined noticeably and consisted of a mere sixteen fellows and seventy undergraduates. His tutor was Rev William Raynes, himself a graduate of Clare, which suggests that it had become a rather inward-looking institution, although he did venture into the outside world as a curate at Witham in Essex. The most notable of Lucas's contemporaries were William Loudon Mollison, who later as an academic inspired a revival in the fortunes of Clare, and three Anglican missionary clergymen.

In 1875 the Chair of Mechanism and Applied Mechanics was established, with James Stuart (1843-1913) as its first occupant. In the Easter term of 1878, Lucas sat examinations for the Ordinary BA in Mechanism and Applied Science – nowadays we would call it engineering – and Stuart gave him a Class II pass.[35] Industry was not highly regarded among the Victorian upper classes, who tended to dismiss its practitioners as 'rude mechanicals'.[36] Lucas was therefore more typical than a later Cambridge graduate in the same subject, the Hon Charles Stewart Rolls of Rolls-Royce fame, in that he applied the mathematical skills he had learnt from his degree to his career as a stock jobber, rather than to engineering.

---

33    Lord Harris, *A Few Short Runs*, John Murray, 1921, p 148
34    This paragraph is based on the Victoria County History of Cambridge, Vol 3: *The Colleges and Halls: Clare College,* 1959, pp 340-346.
35    Cambridge University Library: UA Exam.L.8, p 112. Four men had firsts and five, including Lucas, seconds.
36    See Birley, *op cit.*, p 198.

At a time when the first-class status of university cricket is under threat, it is easy to forget how important it was in Lucas's time. Cricket was played at Cambridge University as early as 1755, and from 1848, when the club moved to Francis Fenner's new ground, its fixture list began to expand with first-class matches against the counties and friendly games against teams like I Zingari. The Varsity match between Oxford and Cambridge was second only to Gentlemen *v* Players on the Lord's calendar, and in the 1860s the rise of the university club contributed to the disappearance of Cambridgeshire as a first-class county. In 1878 Cambridge University won all eight of their matches, so were comfortably the best English first-class side, and they remained among the strongest in the country for the rest of the century.

In April 1875, Lucas played in the traditional Freshmen's match at Fenner's, where the new pavilion had been completed a month earlier.[37] He scored 66 and eight, being twice bowled by R.P.Stedman, who did not go on to make a name for himself as a cricketer. Lucas played two matches for the First XI against the Next XVI without success, but had done enough to go straight into the university side. Against an England XI that featured W.G.Grace, George Ulyett, William Mycroft and C.I.Thornton, he opened the innings and made 47 out of 96. On a high-scoring first day, the Gentlemen of England made 262 and Cambridge closed on 111 for 0 with Lucas on 48, but the next day he had exams in the morning and when he returned after lunch he did not add to his score.

With 58 runs and four catches against Surrey, Lucas kept his place for the Varsity match. Twenty years later[38] he recalled: 'The first match against Oxford in which I played was the one in which we were beaten by six runs, chiefly because of some remarkable bowling by A.W.Ridley. I was out before the exciting part of the match began.' Ridley, the captain, brought himself on to bowl his lobs with only 14 needed, and took two of the last three wickets. Lucas was a relative failure, scoring only 19 and 5. With 232 runs in ten completed innings but no fifties, he made a respectable but not outstanding start for the university.

Once again Lucas batted well for the Gentlemen of the South, this time against the Players of the South; he made 63, his maiden first-class fifty, out of 338 and the Gentlemen won by an innings and 129 runs. Evidently this experience was valuable and in August 1875, Surrey selected him for five games. Against Yorkshire he 'hit freely' for 39 and his best score was 50 against Middlesex but, after Nottinghamshire's Fred Morley bowled him for three and one, he was omitted from the last game. Morley dismissed Lucas 17 times, more than any other bowler. Curiously, the reverse was also true, Lucas dismissing Morley five times and nobody else more than four. Morley bowled left-arm fast-medium, a type of bowling that seems often to have caused Lucas difficulties.

---

37    Details of internal games from C.U. Library: Match Book 1823-1889, CUCC I/2.
38    *Chats on the Cricket Field*, in *The Cricket Field* magazine, June 1893.

In 1876, for Cambridge, Lucas began in good form and scored consistently throughout a season blessed with fine weather. Against an England XI that again included Grace, he made 105, his maiden first-class century in the first innings, and 53 in the second, but Grace's cousin W.R.Gilbert scored 205 not out and the match was drawn. Unusually, Lucas made his 54 against MCC at more than a run a minute, but in the second innings of the match against Surrey 'the most prominent feature of the play was the staying power evinced by Mr Lucas': he made an unbeaten 43 out of 133, a performance whose value was emphasised when the county were all out for 40 and lost by 148 runs.

It was Uppingham's year in the Varsity match. After Oxford won the toss, W.S.Patterson and H.T.Luddington, with five wickets each, bowled them out for 112. Opening the Cambridge reply, Lucas made 67 and *The Times* commented: 'A finer played innings than that of Mr Lucas is seldom witnessed.' With the fourth Uppingham man, D.Q.Steel, he added 67 for the fourth wicket. When they were out, Patterson scored his only first-class century, 105 not out in 158 minutes. Luddington and Patterson reduced Oxford to 60 for five and only a captain's innings from William Game enabled them to set Cambridge 73 to win. Lucas made 23 not out and drove the winning four in a nine-wicket victory. He headed the university batting averages with 507 runs at 50.70.

Lucas's reward was election as a member of MCC. He was selected for the full Gentlemen's teams in the matches at The Oval and Prince's, although he did not play in the Lord's game, which was the biggest of the season. His best innings was 35 at Prince's, in a low-scoring match that the Gentlemen won by five wickets. For Surrey, he made just three appearances and his 64 against MCC was his only innings of substance.

The annual elections for officers of the Cambridge University Cricket Club took place each November.[39] Lucas had been voted on to the committee in 1875 and a year later was elected assistant treasurer in succession to Patterson, who became captain. The president and treasurer had for many years been Rev Arthur Ward, who was the driving force behind the club, but the post of assistant was far from a sinecure. The club had major outgoings such as rates levied by public bodies, tradesmen's bills and wages for groundsmen and professionals. The main sources of income were subscriptions (one guinea) and gate money, which was charged even in the pre-season trial matches. The assistant treasurer, along with the president, secretary and captain, also arranged the matches and selected the teams.

In 1877 Lucas was therefore one of the senior players. The Freshmen's match was between Mr Lucas's side and Mr Patterson's side, the two captains batting at eleven; Lucas was not out for two and 38, and his team won by 176 runs. After starting the Cambridge season with one run in three innings, Lucas came into his own with 90 against the Gentlemen, 76 against Surrey and 95 against MCC. A month before the Varsity match, MCC had

---

39      Committee details from C.U.Library: 'President's Book', CUCC II/9.

# Lord's  Ground.

*N.B. Patterson, Lucas,*
*Steel & Luddington*
*are old Uppingham*
*Boys!!*

## OXFORD V. CAMBRIDGE.

### MONDAY and TUESDAY, JUNE 26. 27, 1876.

| OXFORD. | First Innings. | | Second Innings. | |
|---|---|---|---|---|
| A. J. WEBBE, Esq..... | c Shaw b Luddington | 1 | c Greenfield, b Patterson | 16 |
| F. M. BUCKLAND, Esq | cA Lytteltn.bPattersn | 32 | c and b Luddington...... | 0 |
| A. H. HEATH, Esq...... | b Luddington | 0 | b Luddington ......... ... | 0 |
| T. S. DURY, Esq......... | cA,Lytteltn.bLuddingtn. | 7 | b Luddington ............ | 25 |
| R. BRIGGS, Esq. ..... ... | b Luddington ........ ... | 41 | b Allsopp ................. | 32 |
| A. PEARSON, Esq ...... | b Patterson ..... ...... | 0 | b Luddington ............ | 14 |
| W. H. GAME, Esq. .... | c Shaw, b Luddington | 4 | l b w, b Greenfield..... ... | 109 |
| D. CAMPBELL, Esq. ... | c Newton. b Patterson | 6 | b Greenfield .............. | 43 |
| V. ROYLE, Esq. .. ..... | c A.Lyttelton, bPatterson | 2 | not out ...................... | 11 |
| C. P. LEWIS, Esq. ...... | c Greenfield,b Patterson | 15 | c Greenfield,b Patterson | 1 |
| H. G. TYLECOTE, Esq.. | not out ..................... | 0 | b Greenfield ............... | 0 |
| | b 2, l-b 2 w . n-b , | 4 | B 5, l-b 3. w 2 n-b 1, | 11 |
| | Total.................... | 112 | Total ................. | 262 |

| CAMBRIDGE. | First Innings. | | Second Innings. | |
|---|---|---|---|---|
| F. J. GREENFIELD, Esq. | b Lewis............... | 1 | | |
| A. P. LUCAS, Esq. ...... | c Campbell, b Royle ... | 67 | *not out* | *23* |
| W. BLACKER, Esq. ... | b Lewis... ............ | 0 | *not out* | *0* |
| Hon. E. LYTTELTON ... | c Briggs, b Lewis ...... | 18 | | |
| D. Q. STEEL, Esq....... | c and b Royle ............ | 24 | | |
| Hon. A. LYTTELTON ... | c Briggs, b Pearson ... | 43 | *run out* | *47* |
| W. S. PATTERSON, Esq. | not out...... ...... ... | 105 | | |
| V. K. SHAW, Esq. ...... | b Pearson............... | 0 | | |
| H. T. ALLSOPP, Esq. ... | b Buckland ............... | 21 | | |
| S. C. NEWTON, Esq. ... | b Pearson ............ | 7 | | |
| H. T. LUDDINGTON, Esq. | b Lewis............... | 6 | | |
| | B 4, l-b 5, w 1, n-b , | 10 | B , l-b , w , n-b , | 6 |
| | Total ................. | 302 | Total ................. | 76 |

Umpires—Rylott and Farrands.        Scorers—Davey and West.

\*\*\* Special Telegraph Wires are provided for this Match, and messages can
be despatched to any part of the United Kingdom from the Travelling Office
stationed in the S.E. corner of the Ground.

*Scorecard of the 1876 Varsity Match, won by Cambridge by nine wickets.*
*The annotation, top right, draws attention to the winning side's four*
*Uppinghamians, Lucas, Steel, Patterson and Luddington.*

bowled Oxford out for 12, even today the joint lowest score in a first-class match. The *Manchester Guardian* warned that their prospects were 'grim', but F.M.Buckland's unbeaten 117 took the game away from Cambridge and they lost by ten wickets, before a huge, 'fashionable' crowd. Lucas's 54 in the first innings was Cambridge's only substantial score of the match: he went in first and was out last. He again topped the university batting averages with 337 runs at 33.70, and also began to bowl his slow round-arm more regularly. This may reflect his more influential role in the club, although he could just have been filling the slot vacated by the departure of the captain, F.F.J.Greenfield, who bowled in a similar style.

Lucas had done enough to earn selection for the Gentlemen *v* Players game at Lord's, which turned out to be one of the greatest matches in the series. At 20 years 4 months, he and his Cambridge team-mate Alfred Lyttelton, two weeks his senior, were the youngest players in the game. After the Gentlemen took a slender first innings lead of six runs, the Players reached 148 for six and then lost their last four wickets without addition. Lucas had scored only 12 but was the most successful bowler in the Players' second innings, with a then career-best four for 12 in 17 four-ball overs. After W.G.Grace and Alfred Lyttelton took the score to 64 for one, the Gentlemen collapsed to 97 for nine with Lucas, relegated from opener to No.7, out for two. Then W.S.Patterson joined Fred Grace and, 'amid great excitement', they compiled an unbroken partnership of 46 to give the Gentlemen victory by one wicket.

Still six months short of his 21st birthday, Lucas was invited to captain a predominantly professional 'England XI' against Gloucestershire at The Oval. He had taken eighteen wickets in his previous three matches, but took only one in this game, putting himself on in front of Edward Barratt, Surrey's professional slow left armer, who was in good form at the time. Lucas was a confident but not arrogant man and he did something similar in his first three-day game for Essex, so it was perhaps his way of leading from the front. A hard-fought, low-scoring game ended in defeat for England by five wickets.

In this season Lucas also found his fine form for Surrey. When Middlesex set Surrey 94 to win they collapsed to 42 for five but, opening as usual, Lucas made a typically sound 26 not out and his side won by four wickets, having scored at exactly one run per over. Then, against Nottinghamshire, he produced his then career-best batting and bowling performances; *Bell's Life* said he made his 115 'in four hours with brilliant hits and splendid cricket', and he also took eight wickets for 66 in the match. Against Kent he did almost as well, with 110 and match figures of five for 24. Though he played for Surrey for another five seasons, they were to be the only centuries he made for them. At Clifton, scoring against Gloucestershire on a difficult pitch 'proceeded at a languid pace' as Surrey took 4¼ hours to make 121: Lucas carried his bat for 36 and his defence was the feature of the innings. Rain on the second day made the wicket almost unplayable on the third, and even Lucas could not save Surrey from a collapse to 53 all out and a ten-wicket defeat. With 832 runs at 34.66 and 34 wickets at 13.82, Lucas had enjoyed by far his best season to date, finishing fourth in the national batting averages and fourteenth in bowling.

In May 1878 Lucas had completed his degree and could devote his full attention to cricket. He again selected one of the Freshmen's sides, this time against Edward Lyttleton's side, but neither of them played. The second trial game must have been one of the most even matches ever played: the Next XVI made 96 and 144, the First XI 98 and 144 for nine, of which Lucas contributed only three and nought.

The 1878 Cambridge team is generally reckoned to be their best ever. In the days before the formalisation of the County Championship, the Press were divided as to which was the champion county, but in this season the university was by some way the leading domestic side in England. As their captain, Edward Lyttleton, and his brother Alfred (secretary and wicket-keeper) pointed out: 'They enjoyed a season of unbroken success, winning all of their eight matches, four by an innings and one by ten wickets.'[40] This was despite the fact that Lucas, who had topped their batting averages in the previous two seasons, was not at his best, because

*The great Cambridge University side of 1878, which won all eight of its first-class matches.*
*Standing (l to r): Hon I.F.W.Bligh, Hon A.Lyttelton (wk), D.Q.Steel, L.K.Jarvis, A.F.J.Ford.*
*Seated: F.W.Kingston, A.P.Lucas, Hon E.Lyttelton (capt), P.H.Morton.*
*On the ground: H.Whitfeld, A.G.Steel.*

40    Quoted by Peter Hatton in *The Undecided Championship of 1878: a Cambridge Perspective*, in *The Cricket Statistician*, 136, 2006, p 41.

of illness. He was, nevertheless, second behind A.G.Steel in the Cambridge batting and bowling averages. His only significant contribution with the bat was 49 against MCC, but against the Gentlemen of England he had a fine match with the ball, taking five for 34 in the first innings and two for 9 in the second. In the next Cambridge match, a twelve-a-side game at The Oval, he took six wickets in the match, in the second innings bowling unchanged with Steel to dismiss Surrey for 43. In the Varsity match he finally did himself justice with the bat when, in the second innings, his 74 was the highest score of the game and his 117 for the first wicket with Alfred Lyttelton by far the highest partnership. He also took two wickets and a catch in Oxford's first innings, and Cambridge won by 238 runs.

In May 1878, Arthur Ward had written to the MCC secretary, Henry Perkins, warning of 'the possible break up of [the Cambridge University Cricket] Club which has for so long kept up high class cricket in this land.' A 'fall of members from 80 to 46 was due entirely to an increase in number of private college grounds', and had led to a reduction in income of £97. Ward proposed that a poll tax on members of college clubs should be doubled from 1s 6d to 3s, but also sought assistance from MCC. Perkins asked for further information from Ward, who replied testily that 'the two Lytteltons and Lucas' did not know the details, but the club 'could not continue its hand to mouth existence.' It is probably no coincidence that Perkins finally agreed to cough up £100 on 15 July, when Cambridge's games at Lord's against MCC and Oxford had brought in considerable gate money, and a hastily arranged match against the Australians promised a further bonanza. Although Ward conducted these negotiations, the Lytteltons and Lucas, as principal officers, clearly played an important supporting role. It was an early form of MCC sponsorship of university cricket, which continues today through the University Centres of Cricketing Excellence.

Cambridge in Lucas's time played seven first-class games a season, and in his four years at the university he had played in every one of the 28 games possible. He must therefore have been greatly disappointed when a recurrence of his illness forced him to miss the Australian game, although he was not greatly missed. His team-mates won by an innings and 72 runs in two days but the tourists, who had earlier in the season beaten MCC in a single day, were down to eleven fit men and doubtless exhausted by a ridiculously demanding itinerary. Cambridge in 1882 and Oxford in 1884 both beat the Australians, but by lesser margins, and no university defeated them after that.

Immediately after the Varsity match, Lucas played for the Gentlemen in two wins against the Players, by 55 runs at The Oval and by 206 at Lord's. His 91 in the second innings at Lord's was the highest individual score in the two games. He recovered from his illness just before the end of the season and captained Surrey – possibly for the first time, although in early games the identity of the captain is not always known. He was able to enforce the follow on but Gloucestershire batted out time comfortably.

# Chapter Five
## The Australian tour, 1878/79

In 1878/79, Lord Harris led a party that toured Australia at the invitation of the Melbourne Cricket Club, the nearest Australian equivalent to the Marylebone club. The tour was characterised by languid intervals of sightseeing and sociability, and contrasted greatly with the fiercely commercial Australian tour of England a few months earlier, where match followed match and the players travelled overnight between games.

Unlike previous English touring sides, it was essentially amateur but some of the leading men were unavailable – most notably the nominally amateur W.G.Grace, presumably because he was not offered enough money. The team was therefore weak, so it was strengthened by the professionals George Ulyett and Tom Emmett. Lucas came down from Cambridge in 1878 and, although he had a relatively disappointing season, the reputation he had gained in the previous two years was enough to earn him an invitation.

The team was said to be strong in batting and fielding, although in fact their catching often let them down and they had no genuine wicket-keeper. They also lacked a quality slow bowler, so Lucas often came on as first change. His *Times* obituary recalled in 1923:

> Mr Lucas was not much of a traveller, but he went to Australia with Lord Harris's team in 1878/79. During that tour he had to do far more bowling than he had expected, the side being almost wholly dependent on Emmett and George Ulyett. How with such limited resources they ever managed to get their opponents out remains to this day a marvel.

Harris[41] later commented:

> A.P.Lucas, who, not claiming to be or indeed being in England a bowler of first-class calibre, became, before leaving Australia, from having to bowl constantly, of quite the first class.

Aged only 21, Lucas was the youngest of the tourists, and he enjoyed what would in twenty-first century parlance have been called a gap year. His father must have been proud that the boy he coached 'on the paternal lawn near Esher' had developed into one of the finest young batsmen in England. Orton Lucas had already lost two of his four sons, so perhaps wanted to give Bunny the experience of a lifetime before he settled down to the world of work.

---

41    Lord Harris, *A Few Short Runs,* John Murray, 1921, p 148.

We are fortunate that one of the party, Vernon Royle, kept a diary of the tour.[42] Royle, who was three years older than Lucas, had played against him in the Varsity matches of 1875 and 1876, and in several games for Lancashire. Although he often mentioned the cricket, his main purpose was to record the whole experience. Lucas frequently accompanied Royle on his various outings, so we have an insight into Bunny's interests outside cricket.

The party left Southampton on 17 October 1878, aboard the *Australia*, a steamship of the P & O line. Lucas shared a cabin with his Uppingham and Cambridge team-mate S.S.Schultz. After a rough passage across the Bay of Biscay, they passed Gibraltar and arrived at Malta late on 25 October, immediately engaging a guide to show them the sights of Valletta. The ship was due to leave at 9 am the following morning, so Royle, Lucas and Francis MacKinnon went on shore at 6.30 and their guide took them to

*Lord Harris's side in Australia, 1878/79.*
*Standing (l to ): F.Penn, A.J.Webbe, C.A.Absolom, S.S.Schultz (later Storey), L.Hone (wk).*
*Seated: F.A.MacKinnon, A.N.Hornby, Lord Harris (capt), H.C.Maul, G.Ulyett.*
*On the Ground: A.P.Lucas, V.P.F.A.Royle, T.Emmett.*

---

42    Quotations in this chapter are from Royle's diary, unless otherwise stated.

'magnificent' St John's Church and the Palace, 'a beautiful pile of buildings'. After a stop at Suez, the ship arrived at Galle, Ceylon on 15 November and the party transferred to the *S.S.Assam.*

On 28 November the tourists had their first glimpse of Australia and went ashore at King George Sound, Albany, near the southernmost point of Western Australia. The party then spent almost a fortnight in Adelaide, where they were 'treated with the greatest hospitality'. Cricket in South Australia was still developing, and in the only match there the English twelve defeated eighteen South Australians by three wickets. Lucas faced the first ball of the tour but made an inauspicious start, being dismissed for 12 and none and taking no wicket in four overs.

On 16 December the tourists arrived in Melbourne and were driven to the Town Hall, where a crowd greeted them with hearty cheers and the mayor welcomed them to the city. After dinner at the Melbourne Club, they settled in at the Oriental Hotel, Collins Street. Two days later, five of the party played in a match against '18 West of England', who were bowled out in 45 minutes for 34, after Lucas had made 79 out of 416. On Christmas Eve the twelve tourists batted all day for 434 against a fifteen of the Melbourne Club, Lucas top-scoring with 107. Royle noted that 'many of us got out on purpose' but does not say whether the game was concluded.

As was the custom of the day, Royle left his card with several prominent Melbourne men who were probably known to him or his family. Lucas may have done the same, and certainly they were both invited to visit 'the Moores', who lived in the then wealthy and fashionable seaside suburb of St Kilda. There were several families called Moore in the area but the most likely candidates are Thompson Moore and his brother James, who were owner-directors of various mining companies and lived at Stradbroke, 71 Grey Street. Royle and Lucas went back several times and took the opportunity to play the recently invented game of lawn tennis.

The first major match of the tour started on Boxing Day against fifteen of Victoria who batted into the second day for 313, although Royle commented, 'Our fielding not at all good.' Lucas, with 33 overs, had his first extended bowl of the tour, taking three for 59. He then opened the batting with Ulyett and ...

> When 146 runs had been scored a capital catch at point by the Victorian captain, Mr. Allee, settled Mr. Lucas for 90 – an innings that was chronicled as "first class cricket, without anything like a chance", and that included among other fine hits "a grand hit to leg, the ball bounding over the boundary fence". Hearty cheers greeted Mr. Lucas's return from the wickets and ... Lord Harris's walk to them.[43]

That enthusiasm was a considerable contrast to events later in the tour. Lucas took two more wickets in the fifteen's second innings but they batted out the day and the match was drawn.

---

43      *Wisden Cricketer's Almanack, 1880.*

The whole party then set off to stay with the Robertson family at their splendid stone mansion, The Hill.[44] The family bred horses and cattle and were described as 'not necessarily great breeders but great organizers and born salesmen.' William Robertson rowed in the Oxford crew that won the 1861 boat race, so would doubtless have had strong social links with some of the tourists. Royle's diary entry for 30 December is typical of many, if slightly more bloodthirsty:

> Got up at 6.30 and drove with Fanning, Lucas and Schultz to shoot at Mr Murray's place, four miles from Robertson's. Had plenty of walking over rocks *etc* but could not get near the wild fowl. Saw plenty of wild geese, ducks, *etc, etc*. Returned to Robertson's for lunch. He had got down about 300 pigeons for our benefit, but after a short time, Lucas and I went ferreting rabbits and got about 30 in a very short time. Went to bed very early.

The tourists got up at 3.30am to catch an early train at Colac, and arrived at Melbourne at about 10.30am on 31 December. The biggest match of the tour was due to begin two days later and, contrary to what might be expected from Flanders and Swann's wonderful *Song of Patriotic Prejudice*,[45] they practised in the afternoon. They did not, however, overdo it: they spent the evening at an Oxford University dinner and the whole of the next day at the races, although to be fair it was very hot.

The match was billed as Lord Harris's XI *v* Australia, but has since been recognized as the third Test match ever. Harris won the toss and, after careful consideration, made the wrong decision: he chose to bat but feared rain and, before play could start, there was a heavy shower. Soon his team were 26 for seven and Lucas, with six, was at that point the highest scorer. Harris and Charles Absolom put on 63 for the eighth wicket but England were all out for 113. Harris's XI reduced Australia to 37 for three, but missed several chances and eventually the score reached 256. Emmett took seven for 68 but had little support from the other bowlers; Lucas was first change but took none for 31 in 18 overs. After a steady start in the tourists' second innings, Lucas was brilliantly caught by Harry Boyle for 13. Only a last-wicket stand by Emmett and Schultz averted the innings defeat, and Charles Bannerman and Billy Murdoch knocked off the 19 runs needed in 11 balls. Fred Spofforth had match figures of 13 for 110 which included the first Test hat-trick, but Lucas was twice dismissed by Frank Allan's left-arm fast-medium.

The match was scheduled as timeless but ended early on the third morning, so in the afternoon Lucas and Royle went over to the Moores to play tennis. Two days later they were invited to a picnic at Fern Tree Gully, later of rather greater cricketing significance as the birthplace of Shane

---

44  *Australian Dictionary of Biography,* online version, sourced April 2009.
45  And all the world over, each nation's the same / They've simply no notion of playing the game / They argue with umpires, they cheer when they've won / And they practise beforehand which ruins the fun!

Warne. In 1882 it was set aside as a place of public recreation and described in a *Guide for Excursionists from Melbourne* as a 'gem amongst the jewels of nature's scenery.'[46] Royle noted: 'The roads were very bad indeed. Went to the top of the gully and had a very fine view.'

On 7 January the party crossed to Tasmania.[47] They travelled from Launceston to Hobart on a single-line train track, and Royle recorded: 'The curves on it are simply a caution, the end of the train in many cases being only a few yards from the engine.' At the Lower Domain Ground, a 'very funny ground for cricket, but beautifully situated', they beat eighteen of the Southern Tasmania Cricket Association by six wickets, Lucas making 26 and 45 not out and taking five wickets. On the first evening of the match, they attended the Hobart Town Assembly Ball and, on the second, Governor Wells' ball at Government House, both given in their honour. On 12 January they returned to Launceston and in the evening went to see a waterfall called the Cascade but 'we had rather a steep hill to climb which was very hard work after dinner'. Perhaps it was all rather too much for Lucas, because in the next match, against Eighteen of the Northern Tasmania Cricket Association, he made a duck. There was not time for the Tasmanians to complete their second innings, so Haygarth in *Scores and Biographies* recorded the match as a draw, but Royle thought that 'as it was only a one-day match we won easily'.

After returning to Melbourne, the tourists left for Sydney and on 19 January stopped off at Wagga Wagga, dismissed by Royle as 'a very dusty place.' It had been the home of Arthur Orton, the infamous 'Tichborne claimant', who in the 1860s had tried unsuccessfully to pass himself off as the missing eleventh Earl of Tichborne. It was only in 1874, after a prolonged trial, that he was found guilty of perjury and imprisoned for fourteen years. Doubtless intrigued by the coincidence with his father's forename, Bunny visited Orton's former butcher's shop at Gurwood Street, but found that it had become a doctor's surgery. Arthur Orton was the son of a Wapping butcher and had nothing to do with Orton Lucas. The small town of Wagga Wagga later became famous for producing a remarkable number of top-class sports players, including the cricketers Mark Taylor, Michael Slater and Geoff Lawson.

The party arrived in Sydney the next morning, and 'were driven in a drag and 4 horses to the Exchange Hotel, Gresham Street, where we were very glad to get a wash, *etc* and a good breakfast. It rained the whole day.' On 24 January began a match with New South Wales. It was pretty even throughout and on the fourth day the home side still needed 110 with five wickets in hand, but 'after lunch our fielding was atrocious, missing several chances', so Charles Bannerman and Hugh Massie knocked off the runs

---

46    From Daniel Catrice, *Victoria's Heritage: The Fern Tree Kiosk*, Victoria Parks Service, c1996.

47    Some of the detail in this paragraph differs from that in Haygarth's *Scores and Biographies*. I have preferred Royle's account because it was written at the time.

without further loss. Lucas scored only seven and 15 but took six wickets, including Billy Murdoch and Alec Bannerman, both bowled. He sent down more overs and took more wickets than Ulyett, who did not bowl at all in the next game and was perhaps carrying a minor injury. In an up-country game, Lucas with eight wickets and Emmett with seven, bowled unchanged and dismissed Eighteen of Bathurst for 47. The visitors responded with 229 but rain washed out the second day and left the match drawn in their favour.

Lucas, Royle and Frank Penn then went to stay with Dr Richard Jenkins, another noted cattle breeder. His home, Nepean Towers, was a substantial two-storey Gothic revival country residence which he developed as 'a centre of social, intellectual, religious, pastoral and agricultural activity'. Because of a misunderstanding, nobody was expecting the three young cricketers and 'we walked on as far as the river Nepean, the scenery was very pretty'. Eventually they arrived and, after lunch, shot over eighty rabbits and 'returned to the Towers very well satisfied with our day's sport'. Ten years earlier a better-known visitor enjoyed the rabbit-shooting when Alfred, Duke of Edinburgh visited after being wounded in an assassination attempt in Sydney, and the social set joined him. There was a small cricket ground nearly opposite the house and 'young Jenkins' – in fact a year older than Royle – tried to persuade them to practise with him. Penn had only joined the tour in January and was happy to do so, but 'Lucas and I kept away'. They went out 'on horseback to hunt young kangaroos … and the dogs killed a couple or so'. They had to leave after lunch and 'were very sorry to leave, as we had enjoyed ourselves immensely'. It was as well that they had this idyllic interlude, for the team was about to become embroiled in one of the most contentious cricket matches ever played.

On 7 February the tourists began their return game against New South Wales. Harris won the toss and sent 'Monkey' Hornby and Lucas in to bat on an excellent wicket. They 'played magnificently' in a partnership of 125, said to be the first-ever century partnership in Australia. Spofforth then bowled Lucas for 51, on which the verdict of *The Australian* was 'A fine exhibition of cricket, he did not give a chance all through.' Ulyett and Harris took the score on to 217 for two but, according to Royle, 'Spofforth cut up the wicket to such an extent with his feet that it was impossible to play.' The last eight wickets fell for 50, but batting was equally hard for New South Wales. Despite a splendid 82 not out by Murdoch, they finished 90 behind and had to follow on. They were 19 without loss when there came what *Wisden* called, with masterly understatement, 'The Disturbance'. [48]

The custom was for each side to appoint its own umpire. The tourists had not taken one with them, so they asked the advice of the Melbourne Cricket Club. They recommended George Coulthard, who was from Victoria and therefore, in the eyes of some New South Welshmen, even more of an

---

48    As far as I can see, en.wikipedia.org/wiki/Sydney_Riot_1879, as modified 27 December 2008, is a thorough, balanced and well researched account of the affair.

enemy than the Englishmen. A 22-year-old all-round sportsman, he had umpired in four of their matches without any major complaint but, when Murdoch was on ten, Coulthard gave him run out. Royle recorded his view of events:

> The 'Larrikins' rushed the ground. Harris refused to change our umpire, as we considered the decision a good one. Play was subsequently stopped for the day, as the crowd would not let us go on. During the row, Harris was struck with a stick, but not hurt. It was a most disgraceful affair, and took its origin from some of the 'better' class in the pavilion.

The civic and cricket authorities and the press immediately apologised but Harris replied that 'it was an occurrence which it was impossible he should forget'. The game resumed on Monday when the last six New South Wales wickets fell with the score on 49, Ulyett taking four in four balls, but that was almost incidental. Harris wrote a letter accusing the New South Wales cricket authorities of conniving in betting that he believed to be the chief cause of The Disturbance, and they responded with an indignant denial. Only in September 1880, when the Surrey secretary persuaded Harris to captain England in their first home Test against Australia, did the dust really settle.

Lucas usually preferred conciliation to confrontation, so it may be significant that, of the tourists invited to play in the 1880 Test in England, he, Harris and Penn accepted, while Hornby, Emmett and Ulyett refused. In 1893 he told *The Cricket Field* that 'everything went perfectly smoothly during the tour, which was none the less enjoyable because it was almost entirely without incident.' The interviewer apparently had The Disturbance in mind, but Lucas seems to have had no direct involvement with the violence on the pitch, and his stonewalling matched anything he ever achieved at the crease:

> No, nothing out of the common. We had to travel by coach a good deal, but the nearest approach that we had to an adventure was when we passed through territory infested by the Kelly gang, who had 'stuck up' a bank in one of the towns that we passed through just before we came in.

While all this was going on, Lucas and Royle did not neglect the cultural and sporting aspects of their tour. On the first evening, at the Theatre Royal, they saw an entertainment called *John Bull*. After the match they and three others rowed to Woolloomooloo Bay and back, probably a total of two miles or so. The next day six of them borrowed a yacht in which they 'sailed all over the harbour and had great fun'. As a result of The Disturbance, a planned match against Australia was cancelled and the tourists returned to Melbourne, which probably suited them because …

> Visitors as well as residents spoke of 'Marvellous Melbourne' which was seen as bustling, up-to-date and 'yankeefied' in contrast with staid and old-fashioned Sydney, sometimes referred to by Melbournians as

'Sleepy Hollow'... Melbourne was easily the greatest manufacturing city in the colonies as well as the greatest commercial and financial centre.[49]

Most went by boat but Lucas and three others travelled overland and 'had some first rate kangaroo hunting on the way.'

On 17 and 18 February at Yarra Bend, the eleven amateurs played a two-day game against fifteen of the Bohemian Club. In the absence of Ulyett and Emmett, Lucas opened the bowling and finished with six for 83 in 37 five-ball overs. On the second day he scored 41 and took another wicket, but injured a hand in attempting a catch and apparently played no further part in the game. The Bohemians had seven men with first-class experience, so there was no real chance that a weak attack could take 28 wickets, and the match ended in a draw. Evidently Lucas's injury was not too serious, for two days later he celebrated his 22nd birthday, playing tennis with the Moores at St Kilda.

The next game started on 21 February against eleven of Victoria. Lucas made 38 out of 325 but the feature of the English innings was Blackham's five stumpings, which included the last four wickets to fall. Four of them were off the debutant William Cooper, who also bowled Lucas for his first first-class wicket. Harris's decision to open the bowling with Lucas rather than Ulyett was justified when the amateur took three for 43 in 43 overs, and he took two more in the second innings. At the end of the third day, Victoria needed 58 to win with three wickets to fall but the Englishmen were 'beaten by two wickets owing to our bad fielding.'

After odds games against Bendigo and Ballarat, to which Lucas made no great contribution, the last game in Australia was another against Victoria. In the home team was Unaarrimin, known as Johnny Mullagh, a fierce advocate of Aboriginal rights, playing his sole first-class game. As a member of the famous Australian Aborigine team that toured England in 1868, he hit 1,698 runs at 23 and took 245 wickets at only 10 apiece. In the tourists' first innings he caught Lucas for six, his only first-class catch. His 36 was the highest score in Victoria's second innings, a 'good display of patient, careful, and skilled batting' that inspired the spectators to collect £50 for him, but his efforts were in vain. Needing only 54 to win, the Englishmen collapsed to 23 for four but Lucas and A.J.Webbe knocked off the runs despite 'some slight misunderstanding ... as to the time for drawing the stumps', which meant that they had to come back for a few minutes in the morning.

In the five first-class matches, Lucas came only fifth out of twelve in the batting averages, with a slightly disappointing 158 runs at 19.75. His greatest value on the tour was perhaps with the ball: he took 14 first-class wickets and, though full analyses for non-first-class matches are not

---

49    Russell Ward, *Australia Since the Coming of Man* (Revised and illustrated version), Lansdowne Press, 1982, p 114. Previously published as *Australia: A Short History*, Ure Smith, 1965.

always known, probably bowled more overs than anyone other than Emmett.

On 11 March the party set off for New Zealand without Royle, Lucas and Penn, who stayed behind in Melbourne. The three played in two odds games for the Melbourne Cricket Club against local Eighteens, but their main intention seems to have been to spend a fortnight enjoying the sights and society of Melbourne, where they were altogether more comfortable than in Sydney. Royle's diary entry for 19 March was fairly typical:

> Walked over to the Botanical Gardens. They are very pretty indeed and well worth seeing. In the afternoon we went over to the Moores. We left them about six as we had to return to Melbourne to dress as we were to dine with Robinson at South Yarra. Dr Ford called for us a little after 7. We drove out and had a very jovial evening.

Throughout his diary, Royle almost invariably referred to men by their surnames, as was the custom of the day, but on 14 March he made an exception: he recorded that 'Bunny and I dined at the Riddells', so evidently use of Lucas's nickname had already spread beyond the Uppingham Rovers.

Royle, Lucas and Penn dined out with a fair cross-section of the Melbourne upper crust,[50] which included the shipowner John Hutchinson Blackwood; the Riddell family of Elsternwick, who later gave their name to a Melbourne suburb; Judge W.B.Noel; Colonel William Anderson, commandant of the military and naval forces of Victoria; and Dr David Wilkie, a pioneer of preventive medicine. They kept themselves fit by playing tennis, walking to most of their destinations and going to several dances. They visited the museum, public library and art gallery, which were 'well worth seeing'. They went with Judge Noel and his family to the theatre, watched the St Patrick's Day procession and attended the Melbourne Liedertafel, a festival of amateur choral music which they 'enjoyed very much'. They finally left Melbourne on 24 March and were seen off by many of their new friends. Travelling via Sydney, they rejoined the rest of the party in Auckland on 1 April.

The tourists left New Zealand the next day and settled into the routine of shipboard life, although the Pacific did not always live up to its name. On 15 April they arrived at Honolulu, where Lucas, Penn and Royle made the most of a one-day stop. They climbed 'an old crater above the town, called the Punch Bowl [and] had a very fine view.' After lunch they 'got 3 horses and rode about 7 miles to a place called the "Pali" [where] the grandeur of the scenery burst out all at once. It was a beautiful view and well worth the trouble.' They reached San Francisco on 23 April and crossed America by train. Royle was chiefly impressed by the many marvellous sights and by the high prices, but made no mention of Lucas on this stage of the journey.

---

50    Information about these people mostly from the online *Australian Dictionary of Biography*.

On 5 May the tourists arrived in New York where, at the St George's Club in Hoboken, they played a team which called itself the United States of America, made up of club cricketers from New York and Philadelphia. The match got a good preview in the *New York Times*,[51] which said that Lucas had 'quite an enviable reputation' as a batsman. Only seven of the tourists played, so the numbers were made up by four English-born men who were living locally. The home side won the toss and batted, but were bowled out for 84. Lucas opened the bowling and took four wickets as did George Lane, a Nottinghamshire man who was working as the professional at Staten Island C.C. Lucas and Penn opened the batting and 'struggled for some time before they got a hit, but the way once opened, one brilliant hit followed another with astonishing rapidity.' Lucas hit two balls over the fence, which counted as six. When he was on 98, Edward Moeran 'sent in a twister which clipped Lucas's bat and was caught by Cross.' He batted for 165 minutes and 'was loudly applauded as he left the field.' The Englishmen won by an innings and 114 runs.

The tourists left New York on 10 May aboard the White Star Line's *S.S.Baltic.* Lucas, Penn, Webbe and Royle shared 'a beautiful cabin'. Royle closed his diary the next day and, after some seven months away, the tourists returned to England. On 26 May, Lucas scored 70 against Cambridge University for the Gentlemen of England, captained by Donny Walker, and Webbe was also in the side.

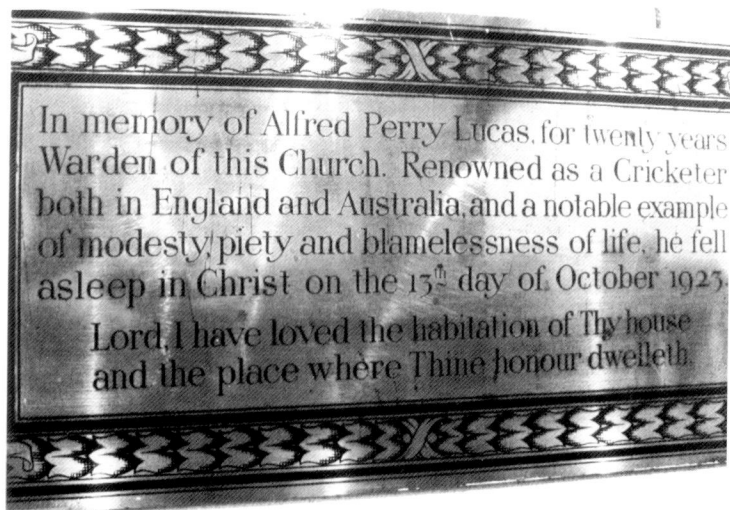

*Though Lucas toured Australia only once, his time there was recalled on the plaque placed in Fryerning Church almost half a century later.*

---

51    From which the match reports in this paragraph are taken.

# Chapter Six
## Surrey and England, 1879-1882

Lucas had been elected to the 24-man Surrey committee on 12 February 1877, a week before his twentieth birthday – a considerable tribute to the respect in which he was held.[52] He was in his third year at Cambridge and was not able to attend a committee meeting until July. It cannot have been a very exhilarating occasion for the young man, because it was chiefly taken up with the bankruptcy of the club's caterers and the eventual taking over of the contract by Ind Coope. Though unable to attend regularly, he was re-elected in 1879 and appointed to sub-committees that were given authority to frame new ground regulations and select ground bowlers. He was also a member of the match committee, which was made up of seven former and current Surrey amateurs.

In 1879 Surrey announced that Lucas, in his first season down from Cambridge, would lead the side – at 22 one of the youngest men ever formally appointed captain of a county club. He did so in their first game, a six-wicket defeat by Middlesex, this time against Donny Walker, but then George Strachan, who had led the side for much of the 1870s, took over again, even though Lucas was in the side. Lucas was not in his best form, but few others were in a wretchedly wet summer. He was selected as usual in both Gentlemen v Players games, but did little. In the second innings of his next game, Kent were bowled out for 38 and Lucas compiled a typically sound 31 not out to give Surrey an eight-wicket win. Despite his committee responsibilities, he did not play in any of Surrey's five Championship games in August, preferring instead to turn out for Uppingham Rovers in their tour of the midlands and north.

In his five games for Surrey, Lucas scored 263 runs at an average of 29.22, and in the national averages he finished seventh with 423 runs at 24.88. He also took eight wickets at 14.62. He was first listed as a member of the Stock Exchange in 1880, and probably started his career there during the winter of 1879/80.

In 1880, Lucas started with 66 for England against Richard Daft's American XI and 34 out of 82 for Surrey against Nottinghamshire, but then had a very poor run of form with the bat. He was nevertheless selected for the Gentlemen against the Players, and had the record, remarkable for a cricketer better known for his batting than his bowling, of taking exactly as many wickets as he scored runs in both games. At The Oval he scored seven

---

52    Details of committee meetings from Surrey CCC minutes: Surrey Heritage Centre 2042/1/3 and 4.

and nought and took three for 55 and, bowling unchanged, four for 26. At Lord's he scored 0 and 2 and, in the second innings, two for seven.

In his next game, Lucas had the misfortune of captaining a Surrey side that was caught on a drying wicket at The Oval and bowled out for 16 by Nottinghamshire. It was to remain their lowest score until Essex dismissed them for 14 in 1983. Perhaps unsurprisingly, Lucas retreated to the comfort of the Uppingham Rovers' tour and missed all of Surrey's six county games in August.

Meanwhile, the Australians were making their second tour of England. They came almost uninvited and Lord Harris wrote: 'They asked no one's good will in this matter, and it was felt that this was a discourteous way of bursting in on our arrangements; the result was that they played scarcely any counties and were not generally recognised.' They were, however, recognised by the crowds who turned out in large numbers to see them, even when playing old-fashioned odds games against local eighteens. The authorities began to realise that they were missing out on a possible money-spinner and the Surrey secretary, Charles Alcock, therefore set about arranging the first Test match on English soil, at The Oval. On 15 July Lucas was appointed to 'a sub-committee for the Australian match with full power to carry out necessary details.' On 12 August this sub-committee reported difficulty in getting together a representative side and Alcock was empowered to pay professionals £20 each, 'rather than the game not be played.'

Eventually a powerful team was assembled, with eight amateurs and three Nottinghamshire professionals. Lucas had played himself back into some sort of form with the Rovers, and batted at No.3 behind E.M. and W.G.Grace. He made 55 off 121 balls 'without the semblance of a chance' until he played on to Alec Bannerman, and added 120 with W.G. – the first century partnership in Test cricket. England dominated the first two days and early on the third Australia still needed 84 to avoid an innings defeat, but Billy Murdoch's magnificent unbeaten 153 enabled them to set England 57 to win. England collapsed to 31 for five before Frank Penn and W.G. saw them home by five wickets. H.H.Stephenson was umpiring and gave Lucas out caught at the wicket for two, although some said the ball came off the pad.

The Test was successful from a financial as well as a cricketing point of view, and the Surrey committee sent letters of thanks to the amateurs, the pros presumably having to make do with their £20. They also passed a 'vote of thanks to the sub-committee for the excellent manner in which they carried out the arrangements for the match between England and Australia.'

In 1881, Lucas picked up where he had left off the previous season. For MCC against Lancashire he carried his bat for 43 out of 126 in 98 overs and for the Gentlemen of England against Cambridge he made a then career-best 142. For Surrey he made 62 out of 110 against Yorkshire and 72 not out against Nottinghamshire, but Surrey lost both games badly. After that he fell away somewhat, but finished his first-class season with 712 runs at 28.48. Again he chose to spend August with the Rovers rather than Surrey.

Not for the last time, Surrey in 1880 enjoyed more success on the balance sheet than on the field, and they lost seven of their fourteen county games. A large sub-committee, including Lucas, was appointed 'to consider the cricketing position of the club'. They proved as effective as most such committees, for in 1881 Surrey lost nine out of fourteen. The County Championship had not then been formalised, but had it been they would in both seasons probably have found themselves below all but Sussex.[53]

It might have helped if Lucas had played more often and had found his best form when he did so. In 1880, five Surrey matches and a batting average of 15 for them were disappointing from one of their finest batsmen, especially as he produced his two best innings of the season for England. In 1881 his six appearances for Surrey included two typically solid, defensive half-centuries, but neither innings could save his county from a heavy defeat, so perhaps his presence would have made little difference.

Lucas opened the 1882 season with what were to remain his first-class career-best performances with bat and ball, for an 'England XI' against his favourite opponents, Cambridge University. His magnificent and chanceless 145 passed his score of the previous year by just three, and was the main contribution to England's first innings lead of 219. Then, after Cambridge had passed 100 with only two wickets down, Lucas took six for 10 in 12.2 overs and the last eight wickets went down for 14; England won by an innings and 92, 'a result mainly attributable to the excellent all-round play of Mr A.P.Lucas.'[54]

Lucas then played another fine innings, against the Australians at Twickenham for the Orleans Club. Charles Dickens, jun. wrote in 1879:

> The Orleans Club was built ... in the reign of Queen Anne. ... It is intended as an agreeable country resort, not only to members, but to their families and friends, and as a rendezvous for members of the Four-in-hand and Coaching Clubs. Orleans House is so called because Louis Philippe lived therein for some years while Duke of Orleans.[55]

The club had its own cricket ground which was 'as charming a spot as one could well imagine.' They played some major teams there, most notably the 1878 and 1882 Australians but also MCC and I Zingari. C.I.Thornton and S.S.Schultz were the best-known men to play regularly for them, but other first-class cricketers also turned out occasionally. Thornton captained the 1882 side, which included the Lancashire professionals Dick Barlow and Dick Pilling, and eight amateurs who played at some time for the

---

53   Indeed, in Roy Webber's 1957 compilation of the table, they were firmly at the foot, having lost more matches than any other side. See Roy Webber, *County Cricket Championship*, Phoenix Sports Books, 1957, p 20.
54   *The Times*, 18 May 1882.
55   In his *Dictionary of London*, see www.victorianlondon.org

Gentlemen. Lucas came in after E.M.Grace was out before a run was scored, and batted throughout the innings for an unbeaten 87 out of 275. *Cricket* commented:

> Some good cricket was shown by the amateurs already mentioned, but the Club would have fared badly had it not been for the brilliant display of A.P.Lucas. His unwearying defence at the outset helped mainly to break the Australian bowling, and his innings of 87 not out, following as it has so closely on his first score of 145 for Mr Thornton's eleven against Cambridge, must be accounted an extraordinary performance; barring a difficult chance to McDonnell at short slip soon after his arrival, there was nothing like a flaw in his batting. For nearly four hours and a half he was combating all the best of the Colonial bowling, and his masterly style was never seen to greater advantage.

The Australians were bowled out for 75 and were on the verge of defeat at 240 for nine when the scheduled third day was cancelled because of the Derby, which says something about the priorities of the Victorian élite and leads one to wonder why nobody had noticed the clash of dates earlier. A few weeks later, in a remarkable game at Rickling Green, near Saffron Walden in Essex, an attractive ground where cricket is still played, G.F.Vernon and A.H.Trevor added 605 for the second wicket and the Orleans Club were eventually all out for 920, both records that stood for many years. After the club was dissolved in 1883, the house and grounds passed into private hands.

The Australians then went to The Oval and once again Lucas was a relative failure for his county, with only 12 and nought. Surrey next had their traditional, high-profile Whitsun Bank Holiday game against Nottingham-shire at Trent Bridge, in which they had to field an inexperienced team with two debutants, while Lucas preferred to appear for Gentlemen of England against Oxford University. He was bowled by the left-arm fast bowler George Robinson for seven and two, but had match figures of six for 56. He played in Surrey's next three games, making fifties against Middlesex and Gloucestershire and 27 not out in a successful run chase against Cambridge University, as well as taking twelve wickets.

But then a letter from 'A Surrey Veteran' appeared in *Cricket* magazine:

> I think also it would greatly add to the strength of the county if Mr A.P.Lucas (to my mind the best all-round cricketer in the world) could be persuaded to devote a little more of his time to his county's interests. Why he should prefer to play *v* Oxford University, when Surrey and Nottingham are opposed to each other, I fail to see. But doubtless he has some good reason for so unpatriotic a performance.

The following week 'A Frequenter of The Oval' replied:

> As regards Mr A.P.Lucas, the 'Surrey Veteran' had better have left him out of his complaints. He is a right-down good fellow, and is perfectly

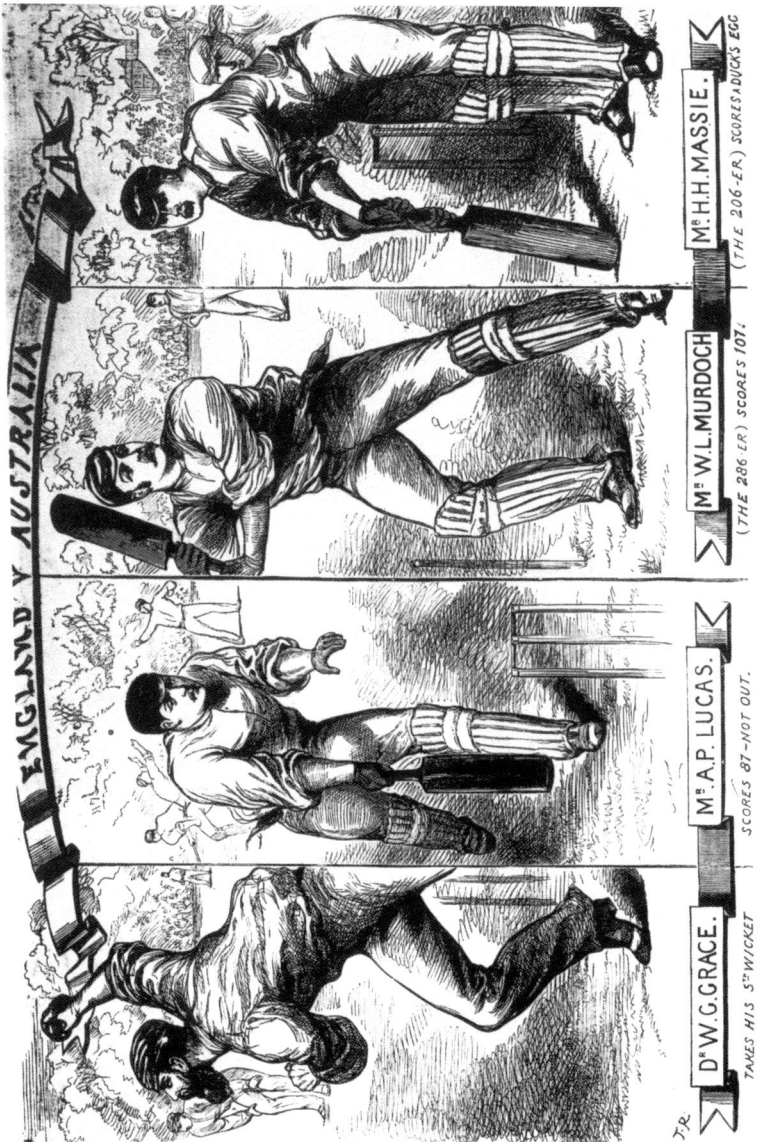

*Four players who appeared in the Orleans Club side which played a first-class match, truncated by the Derby, against the Australians at Twickenham in May 1882. Nine Orleans' players appeared in Test cricket and some of the press billed the side as 'England'.*

justified in playing for whom he pleases. So much the better for Surrey when they get him!!

But it seems that Surrey Veteran's tactless letter had an effect opposite to that intended, for Lucas played in only one of Surrey's fourteen remaining games. At the AGM on 20 May 1882 he had been re-elected to the committee, but only five weeks later the Surrey minutes recorded that he had resigned and the secretary had written to express the committee's regret. There is no direct evidence that the letter brought about his resignation, but it seems likely that the two events were related.

Lucas would probably have missed some of those games anyway, because he played against the Australians for the Gentlemen of England and for MCC. Though 45 for MCC was his only significant contribution with the bat, in the game for the Gentlemen he held a memorable running catch from a 'tremendously hard and low' hit by George Bonnor, which Grace considered 'as fine as anything I have ever seen.'

Lucas played for the Gentlemen against the Players in both games. At The Oval at the start of the second day he went 64 minutes before he made his first run, the earliest known instance of a player batting for an hour without scoring, and yet another example of his unwearying defence.[56] By contrast, his 107 in a comfortable win at Lord's was a sparkling innings in which he added 204 at a run a minute with C.T.Studd. 'Pavilion Gossip' in *Cricket* commented:

It was a very great performance of Messrs A.P.Lucas and C.T.Studd to put on as they did 204 runs for the Gentlemen against the Players at Lord's on Monday on the fall of the second wicket. This is one run more than Messrs W.G.Grace and A.J.Webbe secured for the first wicket of the Gentlemen in the same match at Lord's in 1875. It is, I believe, only twice on record that two amateurs have each made a hundred in one innings of this particular match. ... Messrs Lucas and C.Studd both played brilliant cricket.

In August Lucas toured as usual with Uppingham Rovers, but broke off to play the Australians again, this time for Cambridge University Past and Present. When The Oval Test started on 28 August he was among the leading batsmen in the country and an automatic choice.

Against the 1880 Australians Lucas had been a hero but two years later, some perceived him as the villain of the piece. He started well enough, sharing with Ulyett in England's highest partnership of the match, 39, although he scored only nine off 64 balls in 65 minutes. But then, in Australia's second innings, he uncharacteristically dropped H.H.Massie at long on, to a groan from the huge crowd, and the big-hitting Australian added a further 17 priceless runs before being dismissed. When Lucas came to the crease in the second innings, England needed only 33 runs with seven wickets in hand, but the pitch was getting increasingly difficult.

---

56    *The Times*, 1 Jul 1882.

Earlier, W.G.Grace had run out Sammy Jones who, thinking the ball was dead, wandered out of his ground to pat the wicket. The Australians were furious at this typical piece of Grace gamesmanship, although Lucas later claimed that one of them 'admitted he would have done the same thing if he had been where Grace was.'[57] F.R.Spofforth, regarded by Lucas along with G.E.Palmer as one of the two best Australian bowlers he ever faced, told his team-mates 'this thing can be done'. *The Times* obituary summarised:

> Possibly he could recall nothing in his career more vividly than the last innings of the disastrous match at the Oval in 1882 when England, after seeming certain of victory, lost by seven runs. He stopped any number of Mr Spofforth's terrible break-backs, but at last played one of them on to his wicket. The misfortune was that, while showing such superb defence, he could not relieve the tension by a hit to the boundary.

In *Chats on the Cricket Field* Lucas described it as 'the most wildly exciting finish I ever remember ... I was in at the critical time with Alfred Lyttelton, and for nearly ten overs he played Boyle without getting a run, while I played Spofforth with the same result.' In 55 balls Lucas scored only a single and a four. *The Sportsman* blamed the England batsmen for playing Spofforth and Boyle like 'so many tailors' dummies', and Lucas was an obvious target for this comment, although it was perhaps rather harsh: 'Country Vicar', writing half a century later, describes Lucas as 'defending with utmost skill.' England lost by just seven runs, and the *Sporting Life* published the famous mock obituary stating that 'the body of English cricket would be cremated and the ashes taken to Australia.'

And the Australians were not quite finished with Lucas. He was playing against them at Scarborough for I Zingari and the giant George Bonnor took revenge for the catch, hitting him for a record 6, 4, 4, 6 off a four-ball over. Edward Lyttelton, who was playing in the game, claimed that the assault began 'with a whack landing the ball sixty yards over the sea wall.'[58] Whether or not as a direct result of that experience, Lucas reverted to the status of occasional bowler and took only another ten first-class wickets.

In its report on Surrey's 1882 season, *Wisden* noted that 'Mr Lucas as usual took part in only a few games, and his average showed a drop of 9 points.' The Red *Lillywhite* annual, edited by the Surrey secretary Charles Alcock, considered him 'one of the best cricketers of the day', but suggested that he 'might be keener about county cricket' and recorded that 'the absence of any invitation from the committee of the Surrey County Cricket Club, with which he has previously been associated, left Mr A.P.Lucas free to assist the county of his birth, his presence in the Middlesex eleven adding considerably to their already great batting strength.' Kingsmill Key, Monty

---

57 Lucas's piece in *Memorial Biography of W.G.Grace*, p 149.
58 Lyttelton, Edward, *Memories and Hopes*, John Murray, 1925, p 80. Lucas's 20-run four-ball over was surpassed in 1886. Sixes were awarded at the time only for hits right out of the ground.

Bowden and Edwin Diver were all talented young amateur batsmen who came into the Surrey side in the 1883 season, which saw a marked improvement in the club's fortunes, so their decision was probably the right one. The rift was unfortunate, but Surrey did not entirely forget about Lucas and forty years later sent a wreath to his funeral.

# Chapter Seven
## Middlesex and a serious illness, 1883-1888

In an era when the privacy of sportsmen and others was respected, the press did not go into the details of Lucas's move from the county of his residence to the county of his birth, although *Cricket* did report that 'The Surrey authorities having refrained from asking Mr Lucas to help the county during the season, he determined to throw in his lot with Middlesex.' The only indication that it may have been rather controversial comes from the Uppingham Rovers rhymester:

> ... There's Lucas A.P., a famed cricketer he!
> Once the pride and glory of Surrey
> It matters not now, the why and the how
> But he's crossed o'er the Thames in a hurry,
> Let them call him deserter who may
> But he'll stick to the Rovers alway
> Yes he sticks tight as glue - that's just what he'll do
> Though the bowlers peg at him all day ...

The break was not really of his making, so any accusations of desertion would have been hurtful to a man of his Christian outlook and equable temperament.

Lucas made a good start to the 1883 season, but from the outset his appearances were more intermittent than in the past. On debut for Middlesex his 29 not out and 97 were a vital contribution to an 85-run win over Gloucestershire. He represented the South against the North, and the Gentlemen against both Universities and the Players. He played only three more games for Middlesex, scoring 63 runs in five innings, and no first-class cricket after 21 July, although he turned out as usual for Uppingham Rovers.

Lucas played his best cricket in the two games against the Players. After two days of absorbing cricket at The Oval, the Gentlemen needed 150 to win with all their wickets in hand. They were expected to win fairly easily, but heavy overnight rain slowed the wicket and made run-getting very difficult. Lucas opened the batting and 'played in his best style' but wickets fell steadily at the other end. When he had made only eight, Lucas was caught at point by Lockwood, but both umpires were unsighted and he was reprieved. If he knew he was out and chose not to walk, it would go against our image of the gilded amateur playing the game for its own sake, but we will never be sure. Scoring was very slow until A.G.Steel 'infused some life into the game' with a rapid 31. When the seventh wicket fell, at 104, all of the batsmen except Lord Harris, who made a duck, had outscored Lucas in their respective partnerships. Lucas then took the initiative but two more wickets fell and 14 runs were still needed when he was joined by last man Hugh Rotherham, his Uppingham Rovers team-mate who had taken six wickets in the first innings. Despite being dropped at long on, Rotherham made 11 and 'amid great excitement, a hit from Mr Lucas brought the scores level.' Then the Players gambled by bringing back Ted Peate, who had not taken a wicket in the entire match, and his second ball bowled Rotherham. The tie – see Appendix Two – remained the only one in the 156 years and 277 matches of the fixture's history, and Lucas was stranded on 47 not out. He later commented: 'I was glad I was actually batting at the finish, because when one is looking on the excitement is almost too much of a good thing.' It was the third time he had carried his bat in first-class cricket, a remarkable tribute to his powers of concentration.

In the Lord's game the Gentlemen batted into the second day for a total of 441, of which Lucas's contribution was 'a careful and masterly' 72. After following on, the Players scored 'at a very rapid pace' and Lucas's catches of the Yorkshiremen George Ulyett and Willie Bates, both at long on off C.T.Studd, were important in bowling them out. The Gentlemen needed 108 in two hours, so Lucas batted rather more briskly than usual and his 51 not out saw them to a seven-wicket win.

Thirty-five years later, in the Grace memorial biography, Lucas recalled an episode from this match:

> I remember ... a new Yorkshire colt Harrison had been so destructive that he was selected for the professionals. We won the toss, and as W.G. and I were walking in to commence the innings, he said to me, 'What about this new fellow Harrison? I have not come across him.' 'He is pretty fast,' I answered. 'Well, let me have a look at him,' was the answer, and having found out that he was going to bowl from the Nursery end, W.G. elected to bat at the pavilion wicket. I never in all my life saw any one ever crumple up a bowler as he did poor Harrison. I never received a single ball from him so long as my great colleague was in. He simply laid in wait for him, punished and snicked him, and I have always believed that that small score of 26 (Peate made him play on) broke Harrison's heart so far as bowling was concerned.

The story sounds authentic and the concern of the kind-hearted Lucas for the 21-year-old professional does him credit, but his memory may have been somewhat at fault – as indeed was Grace's, who had played against George Harrison for MCC only seven weeks earlier. Bowling very fast, Harrison had taken 43 wickets in his first eight first-class matches, and in the remaining twelve of 1883 took a further 57. The real blow to his career came in the following season, when he was injured throwing in from the deep so had to cut his pace to medium-fast, and was never as effective again.

In 1884 Lucas played no cricket until 26 June, which may well have been due to the death on 11 June of his sister Fanny, closest of his siblings to him in age. It is perhaps an indication of the respect in which he was held that he went straight into the deep end with four representative appearances – three for the Gentlemen and then a Test match against Australia. His highest score was only 37, against the Players at The Oval, when 'he played in his usually excellent style' for over two and a half hours; he added 86 with W.G.Grace and was seventh out at 153, but the Players won by nine wickets.

Lucas's best performance was perhaps in the Test at Old Trafford.[59] After the first day was lost to rain, England won the toss but soon collapsed to 45 for four, when Lucas joined Arthur Shrewsbury. The bowling and fielding were tight, so batting was not easy, but their partnership was the highest of the innings. Contrary to the usual image of the carefree amateur and the dour professional, it was Shrewsbury who played the strokes and Lucas who defended doggedly, scoring four singles in 24 overs. When Lucas drove Spofforth to the on-boundary for his only four, there was 'plenty of cheering' which was perhaps ironical. He 'never seemed puzzled by the bowling, but he could not force the game.' Shrewsbury was out just before lunch, when the sun came out and made the pitch even more difficult. The slow scoring 'did not tend to increase the excitement', and Lucas made one in nine overs. England lost their last six wickets for 12 and were all out for 95, leaving Lucas 15 not out.

Australia were bowled out for 182 at 1.10 on the third day, leaving England to bat out the rest of the day to save the game. It was a situation tailor-made for Lucas's defensive skills, and he was promoted to open with W.G.Grace. *Bell's Life* commented: 'I don't think I have seen anything finer in cricket for a long time than the defence shown against the superb bowling of Giffen and Spofforth.' With the score at six, Lucas gave a difficult chance at the wicket off Spofforth, but Blackham dropped it. After Grace and George Ulyett were out, 'Lucas recovered the drooping spirits by hitting Palmer well to the leg boundary, the half-century being completed at a quarter to 4.' With the score on 70, Lucas fell to a fine ball from Giffen that broke back a long way on to the leg stump, and just removed the bails. 'His two-hour 24 was obtained by patience and good play, and included 2 fours, 3 threes and 4 twos. Apart from one chance his innings was absolutely free from fault, and he seemed thoroughly to enjoy playing the good bowling.' The game was still far from safe but England managed to bat out time to close on 180 for nine.

Lucas then made his only two appearances of the season for Middlesex. After two failures against his former county, Surrey, he again came up against the Australians. In the first innings his old adversary Spofforth bowled him with a superb ball that just clipped the bails, and Middlesex

---

59    Match summary from CricketArchive: *1884 1st Test Eng v Aus: What the Papers Said of the England 2nd innings*, by John Kobylecky.

*Hedged about.*
*The England side in Lucas's fifth and final Test match, at Lord's in July 1884.*
*Standing (l to r): C.K.Pullin (umpire), E.Peate, A.P.Lucas, Hon A.Lyttelton (wk),*
*A.Shrewsbury, F.H.Farrands (umpire).*
*Seated: A.G.Steel, Lord Harris, W.G.Grace (capt), W.W.Read, G.Ulyett.*
*On the ground: S.Christopherson, R.G.Barlow.*

were all out for 53. In the second he was going well, on 26, when he was run out after poor calling by his partner, Timothy O'Brien, and the Australians went on to win by an innings and 29 runs.

Three days later Lucas was again playing at Lord's against the tourists, for England in the Second Test. After Australia made 229, he opened with W.G.Grace and was brilliantly caught by Bonnor off Palmer for 28. A superb 148 by A.G.Steel helped England win by an innings and five runs, so Lucas was not needed again. He was invited to play in the Third Test but 'could not get away', almost certainly because of his father's death on 7 August. Later in August Lucas played twice more against the Australians, with little success. For Cambridge University Past and Present, he was twice dismissed by Spofforth, for nought and three. For the South, in the first innings he 'played in excellent style' but was out for 28, and then made only five as the South were bowled out twice in a day. It was to be almost three years before he played first-class cricket again.

The *Lillywhite* annual and *The Doings of the Uppingham Rovers* both refer to the ill-health that kept Lucas out of first-class cricket for the whole of 1885 and 1886, when he was in his late twenties and would otherwise have been reaching the peak of his career. There is no indication of what was wrong with him, but having lost his brother William at 30 and his sister Fanny at 29, the 28-year-old must have been greatly relieved to recover

*The Cambridge University Past and Present side
which played the Australians at Hove in 1884.
Standing (l to r): J.E.K.Studd, F.E.Lacey, H.Whitfeld, H.B.Steel.
Seated: W.E.Roller, A.P.Lucas, Hon A.Lyttelton (capt and wk), A.G.Steel,
A.F.J.Ford.
On the ground: C.H.Allcock, P.H.Morton.*

from what was obviously a serious illness. After he and Bessie Luckraft married in September 1885, they had their honeymoon in Australia, a destination which would doubtless have benefited his health. They travelled on the *Liguria*, a steamship of the Orient Line which was owned by C.E.Green, who probably arranged and paid for the trip.

Even though he had been out of first-class cricket for over two years, Lucas in February 1887 received a letter from Lord Hawke, asking whether he could tour Australia with G.F.Vernon's team the following winter.[60] 'It will be great fun if we can get a good lot of fellows together,' Hawke commented, so evidently Lucas was wanted for his social as well as his cricketing skills. His health can only have benefited but he did not go, so presumably he was well on the way to recovery and the demands of business took precedence.

Lucas returned to first-class cricket for Middlesex against Nottinghamshire at Lords on 9 June 1887. *Cricket* noted that he had been 'an absentee from cricket for the last two years', and added that 'he batted with all his own care and judgment.' He top-scored in both innings and played well for 47 in

---

60    Martin-Jenkins, Christopher, *Cricket: A Way of Life*, Century, 1984, p 35.

Middlesex's next game, against Kent, so showed what Middlesex had been missing. With his old ally, W.G., he had an unbroken partnership of 101 to give MCC a ten-wicket win in a twelve-a-side match against Cambridge University, but he failed twice against Surrey at the end of June and played only one more first-class game in the season. His average of 25.33 left him fourth in the Middlesex batting averages.

In 1888 Lucas played only three first-class games. On 17 and 18 May for the Gentlemen of England against Cambridge University, usually a game where he did well, he 'batted with all his old style' but made only four and 20. On 24 and 25 May he made six and 14 against Yorkshire for Middlesex, who nevertheless won by nine wickets. *The Times* report of Middlesex's next game, against Kent, said Middlesex 'did not play Mr A.P.Lucas', which is slightly ambiguous, and of the following game, against Gloucestershire, *The Times* quite clearly stated that he was 'unable to play'.

The Yorkshire game was to be his last for the county of his birth, and *Wisden* commented that he appeared only once for Middlesex 'in a season when his steadiness on bad wickets would have been invaluable'. It gave no reason and even now possible explanations can only be speculation. Work commitments probably increased, and his health may still have been slightly delicate. He had succeeded C.E.Green as secretary and captain of the Uppingham Rovers, which would have taken up more time than just their short touring season. His joining Middlesex was perhaps rather a matter of convenience on both sides: he played only six games for them before his illness and five after, so may not have felt any great commitment to them. If so, it could have contributed to his decision to qualify by residence for Essex which, under the rules applying at the time, meant that he could not play for Middlesex.

Lucas's only other match in 1888 was on 23-25 July for Cambridge University Past and Present against the Australians at Leyton, a fixture first played there in 1886. On a difficult wicket, Cambridge batted first and Lucas's performance belied the fact that he had not played for two months. Opening the innings, he made exactly 50 out of 137. On the second day the wicket eased out and the Cambridge fielding was below standard so the Australians posted 319 in which Lucas, the eighth bowler tried by C.I.Thornton, took two for seven in five overs. Although Cambridge closed 160 behind, 'there was every prospect of an interesting day's play' but the weather was so bad that the game was abandoned.

None of Lucas's four Uppingham and Cambridge team-mates played first-class cricket after 1887, and it would have been no surprise if he too had given up the game. Instead, his cricket career was about to take a new direction that was indicated by the match at Leyton, and this is a good place to take stock of his life outside cricket.

# Chapter Eight
## Stock Exchange agent, 1880-1923

Though several of Lucas's family and friends were clergymen and he was a devout Christian, he chose not to go into the church. Instead, in 1880, he became a jobber on the London Stock Exchange.[61] At Cambridge his degree was in mechanics and he had been assistant treasurer of the University Cricket Club, so he was clearly good with figures and financial matters.

A revolution in communications, first with the telegraph and then the telephone, meant that, from around 1850 to the outbreak of World War I, the City was the economic heart of the world, and London's Stock Exchange comfortably the biggest and most important. In 1850 the largest group of securities had been the government's British Funds, but the Exchange expanded so rapidly that, while they retained their value, their proportion of the whole market fell from 70 per cent to 9 per cent. From 1880 onwards the largest single category was railway stocks, many American, which by 1913 had risen to 38 per cent of a much larger whole.

Members of the London Stock Exchange made a vital contribution to the functioning of international and national markets. They helped encourage enterprise by acting as the central agents in a securities market that brought together potential investors and businesses needing to raise capital, while the international market formed an important safety valve against economic instability at home. They had long taken great pride in their ability to regulate themselves, as indicated by their motto *Dictum Meum Pactum* (My word is my bond).

Yet the organisation Lucas joined was at a crossroads in its history. In 1867 the Council of the Stock Exchange authorised the raising of loans to finance a railway in the Central American republic of Honduras, which the most elementary enquiries would have shown to be hopelessly unsound. It was this 'dishonesty magnificent in its proportions' that inspired Anthony Trollope's wonderful novel *The Way We Live Now*, which described the rise and fall of the shady financier Augustus Melmotte.

The outcome of the scandal was a Royal Commission into the Stock Exchange, whose report in 1878 gave a detailed and reliable account of the workings of the Exchange. It described a flourishing and prosperous

---

61    Details of Lucas's Stock Exchange career taken from *List of Members of the Stock Exchange,* 1884-1924, and from Kelly's London directories. Background on Stock Exchange from: Michie, R.C., *The London and New York Stock Exchanges: 1850–1914,* Allen and Unwin, 1987 and from Reader, W.J., *A House in the City: A Study of the City & the Stock Exchange based on the records of Foster and Braithwaite 1825–1975*, B.T.Batsford, 1980.

institution that nevertheless had a dubious reputation. Often speculation was no better than gambling, so members and outsiders frequently tried to recoup their losses with increasingly desperate risks and eventually went bankrupt. Despite the Commission's trenchant criticisms, it eventually reached a classic Victorian *laissez–faire* conclusion:

> The Stock Exchange is a voluntary institution that ... can hardly be interfered with by Parliament without losing that freedom of self-government which is the very life and soul of the institution. ... So long as the Stock Exchange has the power of expelling one of its members without appeal or redress, it can be bound by no law which it does not choose to obey.

A century and more later, little had changed.

One of the Commission's members complained about 'the very easy admission of a great many young men from the West end of the town ... who go and play lawn tennis and tell their friends "I can put you on to a good thing ... ".' Recruitment was mostly from a narrow band of public school and university men, whose socially acceptable backgrounds were as important as any financial skills they may have had. They were just as likely to strike a deal at a country-house weekend or in a Mayfair drawing-room as in their offices. Many were also keen and celebrated sportsmen whose abilities were business assets, so Lucas's reputation as a cricketer will have done him no harm, and may partly explain why in August he preferred to play for the Uppingham Rovers rather than Surrey. A public school and university sportsman with a socially acceptable background, he was in every way a typical Stock Exchange agent.

In 1880 there were just over 2,000 members, but by 1908 there were 5,000, of whom 2,000 were jobbers. Since 1847 the London Stock Exchange had enforced a strict distinction between brokers and jobbers. The rule was designed to ensure fair and competitive pricing, by forcing the broker to deal through a jobber rather than quote his own price to the client. Brokers were approached by institutions or individuals wanting to buy stocks and shares, but could not buy and sell on their own account and made their money on commission. Jobbers could not deal directly with the public, but quoted a buying and selling price for securities, and made their income from the difference between the two. A crucial change came after 1880, when the invention of the telephone meant that overseas and provincial brokers were able to go straight to the jobber or broker of their choice, and the strict demarcation between the two began to break down.

Lucas may have served a brief apprenticeship with another firm, but by 1881 he was working on his own account at 3 Copthall Buildings, five minutes walk from the Stock Exchange and, unsurprisingly, home to several similar businesses. At No.2 was S.S.Schultz, Lucas's team-mate at Uppingham and Cambridge and on the Australian tour, who was the son of a Liverpool stockbroker. Even now the area of narrow, twisting alleyways has a slightly Dickensian feel, although the stock agents have gone.

*The young stock jobber in 1883.*

'Country Vicar' says that although one of the 'key-men', Lucas was 'unable to make the journey' in Bligh's Cambridge-dominated side to Australia in 1882-3 to 'recover The Ashes.' This was almost certainly because he now had a living to earn.

In 1884, perhaps as a result of his illness, Lucas went into partnership with Leonard H. Gramshaw, and in 1887, briefly, with Frederick W. Crookshank. Both were young men of about his age and, apparently by coincidence, the sons of general practitioners. For ten years from 1888 he worked alone and his firm was formally known as A.P.Lucas. The entry for his profession on the 1891 census says 'stock agent jobber' with 'broker' clearly crossed out, so evidently he preferred to maintain the distinction.

From 1898 Lucas was listed as a partner in the firm of Booth Brothers at 77 Cornhill. When in 1904 Frank Booth left, Lucas and Horace Booth became senior partners and were joined by Arthur Warren Whitefield and Arthur Gastrell Dear. Lucas made his will in that year and appointed Dear as executor along with Herbert Whitfeld, the best man at his wedding and no relation to Whitefield. In 1907, the firm split with Lucas and Dear setting up A.P.Lucas and Co, and Booth and Whitefield establishing H.Booth and Co. This may have been related to a move by the Stock Exchange to revive the differentiation between brokers and jobbers, for their offices were only a few doors apart in Copthall Avenue. In 1906 Booth Brothers had installed the telephone, and the two firms continued to share the same telephone number, but by 1910 Horace Booth's firm was no longer listed separately, and he joined A.P.Lucas and Co. In 1909 the Exchange formally re-imposed the artificial barrier between brokers and jobbers, resulting in a loss of flexibility which eroded its role as an efficient and competitive market.

Sometimes, Stock Exchange firms entered into closer arrangements with the companies whose shares they sold, and were shown in the *List of Members of the Stock Exchange* as partners with them. Early in the 1900s Booth Brothers went into partnership with the Western Australian Land Company, which had been established in the 1840s to develop the new colony and had a reliable reputation as a sound investment. A decade later A.P.Lucas and Co entered into a similar partnership with a new company called the North-West Corporation, but there is some evidence that it was an error of judgment which clouded Lucas's last years. On 12 September 1913 the company was floated on the Stock Exchange, with shares sold at a premium of 10% above the face value to give the impression that it was an exceptionally good investment.[62] It also issued what appeared to be a prospectus, but included in small print the phrase 'for information only', which meant that the promoters could not be held to any statements made in it. It was one of a succession of companies set up to exploit the resources of some of the remoter parts of the British Empire, in this case the gold of the Klondike in Canada. The principal promoter was Herbert Hoover, the engineer and businessman who later became the United States president in the years of the Great Depression, but after two years the Corporation was $70,000 in debt and on 4 May 1917 went into 'friendly receivership'.

C.E.Green died on 4 December 1916, in the darkest days of the war. He was ill for some months and refused, when he knew he was dying, to see even Lucas, although on 17 November he did add a codicil to his will, leaving £500 to 'my very dear old friend and associate for many years in the cricket field Alfred Perry Lucas ... which I hope he will accept as a small token of my sincere affection and in memory of our many years friendship.' He also left to 'my dear old brother Major George Frederick Green [£1,300] which I believe to be the amount which he lost through his unfortunately giving up his underwriting at Lloyds at the time he did.' Green did not mention Lucas in his original will made only three years earlier, so he may have made the similar bequest to him as a result of losses in the North-West Corporation affair.

The Stock Exchange had been closed on 27 July 1914, as a result of the crisis that led to the outbreak of World War I. It did not reopen until January 1915 when Edward Arthur Crowley and Joseph Antoine Last, two experienced agents who had been working independently, became partners in A.P.Lucas and Co. In 1917 Lucas reverted to working on his own and for the next three years only his home in Ingatestone was listed, and no address in the City. Then in 1920, he again took an office in London, round the corner from Copthall Avenue at Drapers Gardens, later the site of the tallest building ever to be demolished in the City of London. By all accounts, he was stone deaf – perhaps a condition inherited from his mother, who was listed on the 1891 census as deaf. In his mid-60s, he would surely have been looking to retire from the Stock Exchange but the continued listing of him and his City office in directories suggests that he did not.

On 12 October 1923 Lucas died suddenly at home of a heart attack, aged 66. For about seven years he had been suffering from angina, perhaps brought on by financial worries. When his will was proved two months later, his estate was valued at £5,490 gross but only £1,238 net. The equivalent figures in 2010 would be about £130,000 and £30,000, so it was a considerable difference. One explanation for this is that he lost heavily

---

62   Hamill, John, *The Strange Career of Mr. Hoover Under Two Flags*, William Faro Inc, 1931. This book is itself strange, a character assassination of Hoover by comparison with which *The Holy Blood and the Holy Grail* is a masterpiece of balanced historical analysis. Nevertheless the basic facts about the North-West Corporation seem accurate.

through his involvement with the North-West Corporation, and repayment of those debts took first priority on his estate.

# Chapter Nine
## The man and the cricketer

If, as seems likely, Lucas did get into financial difficulties, the conscientious way in which he attempted to meet his obligations was of a piece with his character, and contrasted starkly with the behaviour of his brother Percy. He had a great respect for rules and conventions, so the orthodoxy of his batting was matched by that of his deep Anglican faith. In photographs he is invariably well turned out, either in smart cricket gear or a well-tailored three-piece suit. Though no pushover in adversity, he was genuinely honest and humble in character. He seems to have earned the respect and even affection of all who knew him, and I have found no one who had a bad word to say for him.

### Devout churchman

An institution even more important to Lucas than the Stock Exchange was the Church of England, which was always a priority for him. In 1880 the Uppingham Rovers reached Brighton at lunchtime on a Sunday: 'No sooner did Bunny arrive at the Norfolk than he went to sleep, and woke not until 7 pm when he went to hear Mr Wagner and was much edified, though he had forgotten the text.' Rev Arthur Wagner was the Vicar of Brighton, a controversial Anglo-Catholic who was also famous for his generosity towards the poor of the town, building some 400 houses mostly at his own expense. Back in Brighton the following year, Lucas made sure he did not fall off to sleep but straightaway carried out his duty of attending church. He then felt free after dinner to go out with the Rovers to listen to the music on the Pier: 'Bunny feeling annoyed that the band did not offer *The Lost Chord*, Tom politely offered him a piece of string as a substitute.'

Lucas's obituary in the *Leytonstone Express and Independent* summarised his contribution to church life in Essex:

> He went to live in Chelmsford in 1887 and quickly became a popular and esteemed figure, not only in sporting circles, but in church work, for he was churchwarden at St Mary's (now the Cathedral) for many years, and later, when he removed to Fryerning, he held a similar office at Fryerning church ... .

> At Chelmsford Cathedral on Sunday morning Canon Lake made sympathetic allusion to the passing of Mr Lucas, recalling how keen and assiduous the deceased gentleman was in his duties as churchwarden. He was also humble and unselfish in everything, and it was a pleasure to work for him and with him. ... Mr Lucas never let athletics interfere

*'Well turned out again', Lucas at Leyton in his early days with Essex.*

with his religious duty. If he had to play a match on Monday, necessitating Sunday travelling, he never left home until he had carried out his religious duties. They all regretted the death of one who was so highly esteemed.

His memorial plaque in Fryerning church described him as 'a notable example of modesty, piety and blamelessness.'

## A universal favourite

Some of this makes Lucas sound like rather a dull old stick, but that was far from the case: he seems always to have been popular and well-respected. In the early 1880s the *Intercepted Letter from a Lady Rover* in *The Doings* said: 'Mr Lucas is such a good young man, and so sweet-tempered', while *Cricket* described him as 'a universal favourite with all classes of cricketers'. In the 1890s, at Essex, the professionals respected him as a cricketer and as a man, and he was also popular with the sometimes rather raucous Leyton crowd. It is unfortunate that his 1893 interview for *Chats on the Cricket Field* is rather wooden and unrevealing, for his constant tributes to H.H.Stephenson make it clear that he loved talking about cricket, and his friends Charles Green and Charles Kortright both enjoyed yarning about the game with him.

The Rovers' chronicler records several anecdotes which suggest that he had a good, if unsubtle, sense of humour. In Manchester,

> Bunny went out to dine on the Friday evening and I fancy dined well, very well. You would have laughed if you had seen him in the room with his arm round his umbrella, stoutly declaring that 'he would not budge an inch from this pillar.' ... You won't believe it I know, but Bunny made a riddle and declared it was his own. I heard him propose it to Royle as follows: 'I say, Vernon, why are you like the Prince of Wales playing cricket? Because you are a *Royle* cricketer.'

## Marriage and a bizarre divorce case

On Tuesday, 15 September 1885, at St John's Church Lewes, the 28-year-old Lucas married Bessie Arabella, aged 26, the third daughter of Captain Charles Maxwell Luckraft.[63] As a lieutenant in the Crimean War, Luckraft had commanded *H.M.S.Euryalus*, and at the time of the marriage was governor of H.M. Naval Prison at Lewes. The best man was Herbert Whitfeld, a colleague in the great Cambridge team of 1878, and captain of Sussex in 1883 and 1884. He was a member of Molyneux, Whitfeld and Molyneux, the leading bank in East Sussex until it amalgamated with Barclays in 1896. The service was conducted by the Rector of Lewes, assisted by the groom's cousin, Rev Arthur Lucas.

---

63    *Cricket* magazine, 17 September 1885.

I have traced no photo of Bessie Lucas, and she remains a rather elusive figure. She was present at Bunny's death, although curiously it took her eight days to report it and newspaper accounts of the funeral do not mention that she was there. In his will dated 1904, he left her a fixed sum of £500 and most of his personal belongings. As they had no children, he made provision for the proceeds from the residue of his estate to be converted into a trust fund for her, although sadly that only amounted to the £500 plus about £330 for his furniture. She outlived him by almost thirty years, dying at Southsea on 7 February 1953, aged 93. She or the family requested no flowers but donations to the relief fund for the floods that had devastated the east coast in the previous few days.[64] Her will shows that she invested the £830 left to her by Bunny in securities, and managed to live off other income, so that she more than carried out his wishes and bequeathed some £3,000 to the surviving children of Bunny's disgraced brother, Percy. The executor of her will was John Francis Whitfeld, son of Herbert, the best man at her wedding to Bunny almost seventy years earlier.

In 1904 came the most improbable, and in some ways farcical, episode of Lucas's life, when this devout churchman and all-round good egg was cited as co-respondent in the divorce case of Charles Pattrick *v* Fanny Marie Louise Pattrick and Alfred Perry Lucas.[65]

Charles Pattrick was born in 1862 at Thorpe-le-Soken in Essex, where his grandfather had been the miller.[66] By 1871 his parents had separated and his mother was living with their five children 'on allowance from husband', a commercial traveller staying with his widowed mother who was 'living on interest'. Charles' father later described himself as a merchant and evidently there was some wealth in the family, although socially they were below the Lucases in the Victorian pecking-order. Fanny Wardroper was born in France in 1869, the daughter of a British army captain, and in 1888 married Charles, who was then a commercial clerk with a gas company. He had become a gas engineer by 1901, when he and Fanny were living in the respectable Essex suburb of Ilford with four children and two domestic servants.

On 17 May 1904 in the Family, Probate and Admiralty Division of the High Court – popularly known as 'wives, wills and wrecks' – Charles petitioned for a divorce from Fanny, with damages and custody of the children. He 'had been informed that during the years 1900, 1901, 1902, 1903 and 1904, my said wife frequently travelled with Alfred Perry Lucas, the co-respondent, in a railway carriage on the Great Eastern Railway between Liverpool Street and Chelmsford and on divers occasions committed adultery with the said Alfred Perry Lucas.'

---

64    *The Times*, 11 February 1953.
65    The National Archive J 77/818/4857.
66    Information about the Pattrick family chiefly from censuses.

On 17 June the court instructed the petitioner to supply, within seven days, details of dates, times, destinations of trains and class of carriage. Pattrick's solicitor duly replied a week later, alleging that the adultery took place 'amongst other times and places in first-class carriages [what else?] of trains arriving at Chelmsford at 6.03 pm, 7.47 pm and 8.41 pm, at Ingatestone at 5.09 pm and 6.36 pm, and at Liverpool Street at 11.45 am and 11.55 am.' The only minor details he failed to supply were the dates on which all this was supposed to have happened, and any other supporting evidence to corroborate the allegations. Patiently, the court gave Pattrick and his solicitor a week to provide the information, and then an extension of a further week. Eventually they admitted that they could give no more particulars. Not surprisingly, on 10 August 1904 the court threw out the case and Pattrick was not awarded costs.

It is hard to know what Pattrick hoped to achieve. In a society where the scales of justice were often weighted in favour of the upper classes, the court might well have thought of a gas engineer as a 'rude mechanical,' even though his was a skilled trade. He would have needed cast-iron evidence against a public school and Cambridge man, whereas in fact he had no case at all. Perhaps he thought that Lucas would be afraid of a scandal and settle out of court but, if so, he seriously misjudged his man. In 1911 Fanny was living at Sudbury in Middlesex with the four children while Charles was living on private means at a hotel in Lincolnshire, so they may well have been separated.

What really happened between Lucas and Mrs Pattrick? Only they could know for certain. It was apparently a coincidence that Lucas made a will three months before the case came on, and left the bulk of his property to his wife. They had been married for nearly twenty years and, even though they had no children, there is no reason to suppose theirs was an unhappy marriage. Censuses sometimes suggest that couples were living apart like the Pattricks, but the Lucases were always together on census night. If he had been unfaithful to her, it would be out of character with all we know of him and he would surely have felt guilty about it. If there was nothing in the accusation, he would have found it deeply distressing, and a great relief when it was dismissed. Perhaps it was a *Brief Encounter* type of affair, in which two people were attracted to one another but kept a very English stiff upper lip in not doing much about it.

## Country house and club cricket

At a time when first-class cricket did not always take precedence over other forms of the game, Lucas and many other leading amateurs, as we have seen, often preferred the more relaxed social atmosphere of country house cricket.

In 1876 Lucas scored 30 and 77 for Uppingham Rovers against the Free Foresters and, perhaps as a result of this, he was invited to play for the Foresters. He made 53 in a seven-wicket win against Warnham Court near

Horsham, home of his unrelated namesake, Charles Thomas Lucas. C.T.Lucas was the founder and senior partner of Lucas Bros, a leading firm of building contractors, whose work included the Covent Garden Opera House and Floral Hall, several major railway termini and many large hotels.[67] Bunny turned out for the Foresters again in 1877 and a report of a game against I Zingari gave an idea of the attraction: 'So ended the Walton week, and each cricketer, whether Zingaro, Free Forester, or County Warwick, left the ground with the deepest feelings of gratitude to Sir Charles Mordaunt for the week's pleasure he had afforded them.'[68]

At Warnham Court, 'the wicket was flawless, the gardens stunningly beautiful and, at their zenith, the sumptuous country house festivals in July were said to rival Canterbury for grandeur.'[69] In 1879 Bunny returned there to play for the local side against the Foresters, and in the 1880s was 'quite content to be wheeled out pretty much annually to help make up the Warnham Court numbers and took a particular toll of the Horsham C.C. attack.'[70] In 1880 a team of eleven Lucases including Bunny and his cousin Arthur beat Horsham, even though Bunny was absent on the first day, presumably for business reasons.

Bunny also played *for* Horsham alongside A.G.Steel.[71] No fewer than four of the Lucas family played first-class cricket for Sussex, and a fifth played against the county for MCC. Though A.P. was not related to them, he knew some of them through Cambridge: in 1877, Morton Peto Lucas was in the XVI and Bunny was in the XI; and in 1881 when Frederick Maitland Lucas was in the university team, he played against Bunny. The two brothers were on opposing sides in the 1882 match where Bunny achieved his career-best first-class batting and bowling figures – M.P. was playing for the England XI and F.M. for Cambridge.

Even after moving to Essex, Lucas still fitted in country-house cricket when he could. Arthur Edwards, who in 1894 served as High Sheriff of Essex, was an Essex committee member. He lived near Waltham Abbey at Beech Hill Park, an Elizabethan-style mansion set in 700 acres where he enjoyed that ultimate status symbol, a well-manicured cricket field in his grounds. He was captain of the High Beech Cricket Club and hosted an annual week of leisurely cricket that 'was watched with interest by the visitors staying at the house as well as by the spectators admitted to the ground.'[72] Among the visiting teams was an Essex Hunt eleven that sometimes included Green and Lucas, although their changing priorities are indicated by their dropping out in 1889 because the game clashed with a postponed county match.

---

67    C.T.Lucas's entry in the *Dictionary of NationalBiography*.
68    Bedford, W.K.R., *Annals of the Free Foresters,* Blackwood, 1895, p 214.
69    Boorman, David, *A History of the Horsham County Cricket Festival: 1908–2007*, Roger Heavens, 2007.
70    Boorman, *ibid.*, p 15.
71    Hill, Alan, *The Family Fortune: A Saga of Sussex Cricket*, Scan Books, 1978
72    *Cheshunt and Waltham Weekly Telegraph*, 5 July 1889.

# HORSHAM CRICKET CLUB, 1880.

## Horsham v. XI. Lucases, Played at Horsham, August 4th and 5th

### HORSHAM.

| First Innings. | | Second Innings. | |
|---|---|---|---|
| C. Sharp, c. C. J. Lucas, b. A. C. Lucas | 109 | c. M. P., b. A. P. Lucas | 21 |
| P. Chasemore, run out | 21 | c. C. J., b. F. G. Lucas | 46 |
| J. Thornton, c. E. L. Lucas, b. M. P. Lucas | 32 | c. A. C., b. F. G. Lucas | 7 |
| F. Oliver, b. M. P. Lucas | 33 | b. E. M. Lucas | 16 |
| H. Cooke, c. and b. M. P. Lucas | 9 | Absent hurt | 0 |
| Shaw, c. C. J. Lucas, b. R. J. Lucas | 2 | b. A. P. Lucas | 3 |
| W. Aldridge, b. M. P. Lucas | 0 | c. E. L., b. E. M. Lucas | 4 |
| R. Thornton, c. A. G. Lucas, b. R. J. Lucas | 3 | Not out | 13 |
| H. Gilburd, lbw. b. R. J. Lucas | 13 | b. F. G. Lucas | 21 |
| E. I. Bostock, b. R. J. Lucas | 0 | c. F. M. Lucas, b. M. P. Lucas | 6 |
| Skinner, not out | 0 | b. A. P. Lucas | 1 |
| Extras | 14 | Extras | 2 |
| | 236 | | 140 |

### XI. LUCASES

| First Innings. | | Second Innings. | |
|---|---|---|---|
| A. C. Lucas, b. Skinner | 26 | b. Skinner | 1 |
| C. J. Lucas, b. J. Thornton | 7 | b. Skinner | 38 |
| M. P. Lucas, c. Skinner, b. Aldridge | 56 | run out | 9 |
| F. M. Lucas, l.b.w., b. Gilburd | 24 | b. Skinner | 21 |
| E. M. Lucas, c. J. Thornton, b. Skinner | 0 | Not out | 77 |
| A. G. Lucas, b. Gilburd | 27 | Not out | 20 |
| E. L. Lucas, b. Gilburd | 0 | | |
| F. G. Lucas, c. R. Thornton, b. Sharp | 0 | | |
| Rev. A. Lucas, not out | 9 | c. Skinner, b. Sharp | 3 |
| R. J. Lucas, c. R. Thornton, b. Sharp | 10 | | |
| A. P. Lucas, absent | 0 | b. Skinner | 27 |
| Extras | 12 | Extras | 11 |
| | 171 | | 207 |

PRINTED AT THE "ADVERTISER" OFFICE, HORSHAM.

*Bunny was co-opted into a family side of Sussex Lucases to play Horsham in 1880. Five played first-class cricket in their time.*

Lucas wasn't just roped in for his cricket, and went out with the Essex Hunt, whose official historian recalled a hunt in 1889 in which Lucas took part: '… we came over a very rough country. Running by Menagerie Wood, through Navestock and on to Dudbrook, pulling our fox down in a covert close to Navestock Heath; one hour and thirty minutes, most of it very fast … .'[73] In his will, dated 1904, Lucas left to his wife 'all my horses carriages saddlery harness stable furniture tools and utensils', so evidently he retained the accoutrements of a country gentleman.

Throughout the 1890s Lucas captained the Chelmsford club, which improved 'mainly through the efforts of its captain … who has always taken a great interest in its welfare.' … [He] 'raised the club to one of the best in the county from one of very modest pretensions.'[74] Its ground was owned by Henry Frank Johnson, Bishop of Colchester, who was rector of Chelmsford when Lucas served as a churchwarden there. In 1893, the club won 14 games, drew four and lost just one. Lucas headed the batting averages with 570 runs at 63.33, and also took 30 wickets at 17.90. In August the club had an annual cricket festival at which, in 1893, Mr Lucas's eleven included his Essex colleagues Hugh Owen and Henry Taberer, and his Rovers chum Hugh Rotherham. In a two-day, two-innings match, Lucas scored 31 and 47 not out in a comfortable win against the Free Foresters. He later moved to the Brentwood club, which played and still plays at the Old County Ground. Among his team-mates there were Essex players Charles Kortright, Frederick Fane and Arnold Holcombe Read, father of 'Hopper', who had a brief but explosive career for Essex and England in the mid-1930s.

## The batsman

Lucas's obituary in *The Times* summarised his style[75]:

> Mr. Lucas was in the truest sense of the word a classic batsman. A master of both back and forward play, he represented the strictest orthodoxy. No doubt if he had allowed himself a little licence he might have made more runs, but his method served him so well that right into middle age he kept up his form. It may fairly be said of him that no defensive batsman of any generation was better worth looking at. He played the ball so hard and his style was so irreproachable that one could watch him for hours without a moment of weariness … .

Two days after Lucas's *Times* obituary appeared, in a letter the Rev Dr Edward Lyttelton, a colleague of Lucas in the great Cambridge University teams of the late 1870s wrote:

---

73    Yerburgh, H.Beauchamp, *Leaves from a Hunting Diary in Essex: Volume II*, Vinton, 1900, p 177.
74    *Victoria History of the County of Essex: Volume 2*, Constable, 1907, p 609.
75    16 Oct 1923. It was reprinted near enough word for word in *Wisden* whose editor, Sydney Pardon, appended his initials so was almost certainly the author.

Your correspondent's estimate of this great batsman is just, save in one particular. Lucas was not strictly speaking a strong forward player, he scored principally from a powerful 'punch' off a good length ball just wide of the off stump; but it was not an off drive. Another superb stroke was his play off his legs. Moreover, there was a serious blemish in his style. When he did play forward, the bat always screwed a little, so that if he miscalculated the pace of the ball – which he very seldom did – he would miss it. This frailty caused him to be bowled by H.G.Tylecote in the 'Varsity match of 1877, after a light rain had disturbed the pitch. Also his style was not 'classic', if that word implies grace as well as ease. But he had real genius of eye; he could follow a turning ball wonderfully and did not know what nervousness meant. Let me add that all through life he was a fine type of a simple-hearted, perfectly sincere Christian, as many of the residents in Essex know.

It is hard to imagine that a 'perfectly sincere Christian' like Lucas would play with anything but a straight bat, but here we have the word of a senior churchman for it. There is also some statistical evidence: in first-class cricket he was, unusually, bowled (176 times) more often than he was caught (169). By contrast, his exact contemporary Arthur Shrewsbury was out bowled 208 times but caught 428. This was perhaps also a tribute to Lucas's method, for Lord Hawke recalled H.H.Stephenson saying that 'he drove the ball into the ground more than anyone else', suggesting that he gave fewer catching opportunities.

Lyttelton told W.A.Bettesworth that he considered Lucas and D.Q.Steel were 'born cricketers' and Stephenson agreed, but also took some of the credit: 'There were many features of their play, including their beautiful stroke of a leg-side ball – so fatal to many – which they would hardly have possessed if they had not been coached.' W.G.Grace concurred that Stephenson's coaching was ...

> the foundation of a batting style that has been the admiration of every first-class player ... [Lucas's] batting was free and correct, and he had great patience. He made the most of his height, and came down the ball with great force; he was particularly strong in driving.'[76]

Sydney Pardon confirmed this in his 1921 obituary of C.F.Leslie:

> I remember being struck one afternoon when he and A.P.Lucas were in together at Lord's by the contrast in their back play. Lucas came down very hard on the ball every time, but Leslie adopted a sort of hanging guard and almost allowed the ball to hit his bat. Both were watchful to a degree, but Lucas was much the better to look at.'

As befits a man with a mathematical turn of mind, Lucas seems always to have been aware of his performances. During one Rovers game at Old Trafford, 'The little man, again paying attention to his average, was

---

76    W.G.Grace, or more correctly his ghost-writer W.Methven Brownlee, in his book *Cricket*, J.W.Arrowsmith, 1891, pp 338-339.

discovered behind the pavilion with a paper and pencil trying to do a long division sum.' Amateurs often showed some disdain for averages, so the comment may reflect mild, if amused, disapproval. When interviewed for *Chats on the Cricket Field* in 1893, Lucas was rather vague about the details of some matches he played in, but knew exactly how many runs he had scored.

It was perhaps Lucas's very orthodoxy that left him in the ranks of the very good rather than the truly great batsmen. He was better at saving matches than winning them, an unusual role for an amateur: by 1883, he had carried his bat three times in first-class matches, none of them in a winning cause. In 1899 'Historicus', writing in *Harmsworth Magazine* commented: 'In his youthful days his cricket, though it delighted the expert, was rather too slow to suit the tastes of the unscientific spectator'. [77]

Herbert Gibson in *The Doings* summarised his outstanding 1881 season for the Rovers thus: 'In getting all those runs he displayed all his well-known patience, his defence was superb and he punished any loose bowling with great vigour.' When playing for the Rovers, he knew that even if he received a few good balls there would be a bad one along before too long, so his patient defence was enough. At the very highest level, as in The Ashes match, he lacked the flair to break the shackles of relentlessly accurate bowling. For the Rovers he averaged 40 and for Essex pre-first-class 35, but in first-class cricket a relatively low 26.

## The bowler

Lucas's bowling was generally described as slow round-arm. It apparently did not spin much so seemed innocuous, but it was probably very accurate and achieved a degree of bounce. The number of victims he had caught and bowled suggests that he employed clever changes of flight and pace.

Early in his career, the extent to which Lucas bowled depended largely on his team's bowling resources. At school he bowled more in 1874, after Patterson and Schultz had left. When he joined them at Cambridge, he initially bowled little but in his last two years there became a useful change bowler.

With the Uppingham Rovers, as for any predominantly amateur side, bowlers were always less plentiful than batsmen, and also opposing batsmen were not as strong as in first-class cricket. Lucas often opened their bowling and remains their third highest wicket-taker. Early in his Rovers career he was described as bowling 'loblollies' and 'in the style called "Cock-a-doodle-do"'. These may be Rovers slang for over-arm lobs, which he definitely bowled later, and for donkey-drops of the sort that so spectacularly deceived Conan Doyle. H.H.Stephenson was an advocate of lobs and may have encouraged Lucas to bowl them.

---

77      Quoted in Allen, David Rayvern (ed), *Cricket's Silver Lining, 1864–1914*, Guild Publishing, 1987, p 383.

## UPPINGHAM ROVERS *v.* PORTSMOUTH UNITED SERVICE.

### UNITED SERVICE.

| 1ST INNINGS. | | 2ND INNINGS. | |
|---|---|---|---|
| Captain Barton, run out | 19 | c Eccles, b Rotherham | 10 |
| A. Conan Doyle, run out | 18 | hit wkt, b Lucas | 5 |
| C. H. Cobb, b Lucas | 1 | b Lucas | 2 |
| C. M. Stewart, b Lucas | 5 | c Roberts, b Rotherham | 0 |
| Rev. Paske Smith, b Rotherham | 37 | b Lucas | 3 |
| C. B. Hill, c Lucas, b Rotherham | 20 | c Steel, b Roberts | 27 |
| Private Hammersley, b Rotherham | 6 | b Rotherham | 20 |
| C. M. Kendal, c Jillard, b Roberts | 0 | not out | 6 |
| F. E. Cooper, b Roberts | 7 | run out | 5 |
| Price, not out | 27 | run out | 22 |
| Col. Kay, c Lees, b Hope | 11 | c Hope, b Rotherham | 8 |
| Extras | 12 | Extras | 5 |
| | **163** | | **113** |

### UPPINGHAM ROVERS.

| 1ST INNINGS. | | 2ND INNINGS. | |
|---|---|---|---|
| A. P. Lucas, b Barton | 6 | not out | 30 |
| S. S. Schultz, c Cooper, b Doyle | 51 | not out | 29 |
| H. B. Steel, c Hammersley, b Barton | 17 | l b w, b Price | 6 |
| J. H. Roberts, b Price | 0 | b Price | 3 |
| J. Lees, b Barton | 20 | b Barton | 0 |
| H. Eccles, b Hammersley | 10 | | |
| B. Hope, b Price | 11 | | |
| J. F. Whitwell, c Kendall, b Barton | 27 | | |
| H. P. Jillard, l b w, b Hamersley | 20 | | |
| H. Rotherham, c Cobb, b Doyle | 0 | | |
| W. F. Whitwell, not out | 0 | b Price | 7 |
| Extras | 6 | Extras | 6 |
| | **16o** | | **81** |

*The dismissal that inspired 'The Story of Spedegue's Dropper':*
*Conan Doyle  hit wkt b Lucas  5.*

Lucas had no great opinion of his own bowling, telling *The Cricket Field*:

> Oh, I never did anything particularly good, but I once in a Gentlemen and Players match took four or five wickets for a few runs. I never remember going on in a match and changing the fortune of the game.

He perhaps was undervaluing himself, because for six years he was quite an effective bowler in first-class cricket. In the English seasons from 1877 to 1882 and on the Australian tour he took 143 wickets at 16.51, but in the rest of his career only 12 wickets at over 40.

## The fieldsman

Lucas told *Chats on the Cricket Field*:

> I prefer fielding in the country. I remember one terrible miss that I made in front of the pavilion at The Oval. It was in the England *v* Australia match ... when we were beaten by six runs. The only excuse I could give is that the hit was low and hard. As Massie afterwards made 30, the miss made all the difference in the result of the match. I once caught Bonnor off just such another low and hard hit.

That drop was a rare mistake but reports on his speed across the ground are variable. According to Green *Lillywhite*, as a 15-year-old schoolboy he was 'rather slow in the field, and very slow between the wickets'. He improved in the following year and by the time he left Uppingham was 'a splendid field anywhere'. When first at Cambridge he was 'apt to be slow in the field' but in his last year there was 'a sure field anywhere'. H.H.Stephenson said that the catch off Bonnor was famous 'because of the distance he ran and the marvellous way, on getting to the ball, he managed to clutch it while still at top-speed.'[78] In 1891 W.G.Grace considered him 'very quick' but eight years later noted, rather wryly, that 'like myself, he does not get faster in the field'.[79]

Lucas occasionally filled in with some success as a wicket-keeper. In his last year at Uppingham, D.Q.Steel usually kept wicket but Lucas took the gloves when Steel was bowling and was described as 'a fair wicket-keeper'. Then, at Essex, he kept wicket in several matches in 1892, in three in 1897 and in one as late as 1904, when the professional wicket-keepers were unavailable. His great powers of concentration and his adaptability as a team man would perhaps have made him suitable for this role, although he preferred fielding 'in the country' and did not take it on regularly. He never made a first-class stumping, although he achieved dismissals that way in lesser matches in 1891 and 1892.

---

78    Gordon, Home, *Some Notable Cricket Bats*, in *The Windsor Magazine*, September 1906, p 453.
79    *Cricket*, J.W.Arrowsmith, 1891, p 339; and *Cricketing Reminiscences and Personal Recollections*. James Bowden, 1899, p 137.

## *Captaincy*

CricketArchive shows Lucas as captain in 32 first-class matches, but the list is probably incomplete. According to Home Gordon,[80] 'Personally Mr Lucas is one of the most modest and retiring of men. He refused the captaincy of Cambridge University, and never liked leading any side.' He was briefly appointed captain of Surrey and occasionally skippered sides in individual matches, but he did not lead a team for a whole campaign until he was elected captain of the Rovers in 1886. The evidence is that, despite any reluctance, for them he was quite a shrewd and tough-minded captain, who stood no nonsense.

At Eastbourne in 1887, when Lucas was either ignorant or disingenuous, he and his side benefited:

> At 6.26 J.Turner was out first ball and Bunny, not knowing the rules of the game, refused to send a man in so there was an argument which lasted until 6.30; time to draw. Next morning Bunny went in and showed he was in form. After a lease at slip he soon made his hundred.

He eventually scored 137 and, in the days before declarations, the later batsmen tried to get themselves out but the match ended in a draw.

In 1888 at Huddersfield, the Rovers bowled poorly and 'Bunny's unspoken but very evident contempt made the Uppingham Rovers bowlers look rather low.' Overnight Lucas had stern words with his leading bowler, A.M.Sutthery, who on the second day took nine wickets as the Rovers bowled Huddersfield out twice. In the following year, the Bradford team comprised eleven professionals who 'damned the pitch as unfit to play on but Bunny stood firm and refused to allow the pitch to be changed, so eventually a start was made.' He proved his point by scoring 96.

Lucas had succeeded C.E.Green as captain of the Rovers and in 1889 took over from his old friend at his new county, where he soon showed that he could be just as stern and competitive a captain. Essex dominated their game at Leicester and were left needing only 45 to win in 65 minutes but 'batted very indifferently' and collapsed to 39 for seven, of which Lucas made 21 not out. Even after the passage of seven years Hugh Owen recalled with typical cricketer's understatement that 'A.P.Lucas was one of the not outs, but he did not look very pleased when he came into the pavilion.'[81]

Lucas led Essex for all but one of the next six years, and his captaincy probably played as big a part as his batting in their gaining first-class status. He was by far the most experienced amateur in the side but, if Gordon is right, it was greatly to his credit that he accepted a role he did not much enjoy. He resigned after the 1894 season but from 1898 began to deputise for his successor, Hugh Owen. After Owen's retirement in July 1902, he was formally appointed club captain for the rest of the season.

80    Gordon, *op cit.*, p 454.
81    *Cricket* magazine, 1896.

Two episodes from that period suggest that he had the gentlemanly approach to captaincy we might expect. At Lord's in 1901 Middlesex suffered injuries to Albert Trott and George Beldam, so 'by the courtesy of Mr Lucas, the Essex captain, Mr Cobb was allowed to come in' as a full member of the side. At Canterbury in 1902, Charles Kortright created a rough patch on to which Charlie McGahey bowled his leg-breaks with deadly effect. 'A.P.Lucas, who was captain on that particular occasion, as soon as he noticed it, thorough sportsman as he is, refrained from bowling Kortright in the second innings.'[82] McGahey took six wickets in the first innings but only one in the second and, although Kortright did in fact bowl again, it could have been from the opposite end.

## An unfulfilled talent?

From 1877 to 1884 Lucas was, when available, an automatic choice for England and for the Gentlemen in the matches at Lord's and The Oval. After that, he played only once for the Gentlemen and not at all for England: his cricket career at the highest level was virtually ended at the age of 27. Gerald Howat suggested that 'In a spasmodic career that covered 33 years, mostly with Essex, work commitments never allowed him to fulfil the early expectations.'[83] His work on the Stock Exchange undoubtedly took up more of his time and, with a young wife to support, he could not get away as often as before, but there was more to it than that. The break caused by his ill-health allowed new men to come through, and he may not have done quite enough to displace them. The aftermath of the illness may have caused a slight waning of his powers, and then his decision to join Essex meant that he played very little first-class cricket until they attained that status in 1894. But for Lucas there was more to life than cricket, and he is unlikely to have seen himself as a failure.

---

82      Kortright's distant cousin Digby Jephson, quoted by Meredith, *op cit.*, p 157.
83      Gerald Howat in his introduction to Royle, *op cit.*, p 4.

# Chapter Ten
## Essex captain, 1889-1894

Lucas's *Times* obituary summarised his county career thus: 'In county cricket Mr Lucas had a varied experience. He came out in 1874 for Surrey, played some years later for Middlesex, and finally in 1889, with the view of helping his life-long friend, Mr C.E.Green, threw in his lot with Essex.' His Warnham Court namesakes and his wife's family both lived in Sussex, so there must have been some possibility that he would qualify to play for that county. It was therefore quite a coup for Green when he enticed such a famous and experienced batsman to the minor county of Essex, although Lucas perhaps benefited from a revival of his enthusiasm for the game, as well as doing Green a favour. In 1887 he signalled his intentions by moving to a house near Chelmsford and turning out for the Gentlemen of Essex, for whom he hit 151 against Shoebury Garrison.

The Essex club that Lucas joined was founded in 1876, on the initiative of James Round, MP for East Essex and Lord of the Manor of Birch, a village near Colchester. Records and newspaper reports of its first six seasons reveal a leisurely gentlemen's club that was largely amateur and amateurish in its organisation. The club's rapid transformation was due chiefly to Green, who in 1883 was elected captain and chairman. Irascible when crossed, but whole-hearted in all that he did, this wealthy shipowner brought to his native county the same charm, drive and generosity that had benefited his old school, Uppingham. Of his many initiatives, the most significant was to move the club's headquarters ground from the then sleepy town of Brentwood to the bustling suburb of Leyton, in the 1880s the most rapidly growing part of the country.

At that time, the first-class counties made no formal arrangements among themselves for deciding the champion county, which was therefore acclaimed by the sporting press, not always unanimously. In December 1889, after a three-way tie in the Championship, a meeting of the secretaries of the eight first-class counties voted to introduce a simple system whereby the points total was calculated by deducting losses from wins.

Meanwhile, other counties were working towards entering the Championship. To encourage this, the newly-appointed editor of *Wisden*, Charles Pardon, published a 'Second-Class Counties Competition' table, starting with the 1888 season. Evidently his ideas gained currency quickly, for as early as June 1888 the *Walthamstow Guardian* referred to 'a match between these second-class counties' (Essex and Leicestershire). There was no formal management committee responsible for running the second-class counties competition and it was not officially recognised by MCC. The results nevertheless contributed to the entry of Somerset to the first-class County Championship in 1891, and Derbyshire, Essex, Hampshire, Leicestershire and Warwickshire in 1895, when the first-class Championship grew from nine to 14 teams.

Until 1889 there was a rule that players could not appear for their old county while qualifying for the new, but apparently it was not enforced very consistently: in the seasons 1887 and 1888 Lucas played five games for Middlesex while qualifying for Essex, although his not appearing for Middlesex after May 1888 may have been due to a belated application of this rule. Whether he would otherwise have had to wait another year or two is unclear. Such rules were sometimes a means whereby county committees exercised indirect social control over their professionals, who could rarely afford such a long break in their earning capacity. Perhaps the rule was changed when the authorities realised that amateurs like Lucas might also wish to switch counties. After stricter rules for qualification were introduced in 1873, he was the fifth cricketer to appear for three counties, and the first prominent amateur. Although there is no specific mention of him in the Essex minute book, the secretary did cut out and paste in a copy of the relevant paragraph.

In 1901 *The Times* commented: 'It is some 20 years since Mr Lucas made his mark as a great batsman, and he was never so keen on county cricket as some of his colleagues in that ever famous Cambridge eleven. He has hovered about various counties – Surrey, Middlesex and Essex.' It is undoubtedly true that Lucas played relatively little for his first two counties: for Surrey he appeared 41 times in nine years, and for Middlesex 11 in five. He was often called on for representative cricket, and in August he apparently preferred the companionship of his old school chums in the Uppingham Rovers.

With his Essex career, however, it was different. In general, the greater formalisation of county cricket meant that many people took it rather more seriously. In particular, Lucas played very little representative cricket and, perhaps more significantly, made only three appearances for the Rovers after 1890. He clearly enjoyed the social side of cricket, and apparently found it with Essex in a way he didn't with Surrey or Middlesex. Doubtless the influence of Green was a significant factor.

## *1889*

Green told the Essex Annual General Meeting on 3 May 1889 that 'The cricket prospects, under the able captaincy of Mr A.P.Lucas, who would play as often as possible … were certainly better than they had been.' Green was in his 43rd year and doubtless ready to stand down as captain, so his old friend was the ideal successor. Lucas's arrival marked an important step in the serious business of attaining first-class status: his class as a batsman and the experience he brought to the captaincy undoubtedly made a crucial contribution to it.

Lucas made a wonderful start to his Essex career. At Green's invitation, W.G.Grace brought a 'somewhat moderate' MCC team down to Leyton.[84] Lucas and his friend Hugh Owen added 185 for the first wicket and 'batted in excellent form, fairly collaring the bowling of Mr Grace, Alec Hearne and Hulme'. Lucas gave two chances but went on to make 103 with eight 4s, seven 3s, and fifteen 2s. MCC followed on but it was only a two-day game and they escaped with a draw. Grace and Lucas stayed with Green, and 'had many cricket yarns and reminiscences that they were able to recall'.[85] Grace wrote to thank his host and added that 'he would like to receive twenty guineas of the advertisement he had afforded the new ground'. His presence undoubtedly boosted attendances and Green sent a cheque – but did not seek to hide his indignation.

Perhaps as a result of this performance, Lucas was picked for the Gentlemen for the first time since 1884, but they were bowled out twice in a day and lost by ten wickets. He opened with Grace and his scores of three and 17 weren't conspicuously worse than anyone else's, but it was his last game for the Gentlemen despite some excellent performances for Essex.

Lucas led the side in all but two of the county matches. Against Derbyshire at Leyton, he opened the bowling in preference to the experienced professional Harry Pickett and sent down 58 five-ball overs, but Pickett proved a point by taking 31 wickets in the next three matches, and Lucas never again bowled as many overs for Essex. Lucas then captained Essex to their biggest win to date against a county, an innings and 123 runs against Leicestershire who 'in an hour and ten minutes were disposed of for 51, and that on a wicket with which no particular fault could be found.' Next came an even finer win, only Essex's second against first-class opposition; Surrey were set 193 to win but 'In an hour and twenty minutes they were all dismissed for the paltry total of 57.'

Lucas could look back with satisfaction on his first year with Essex. As captain, he led them to wins over Leicestershire and Surrey that were among the best in the club's brief history. As batsman, he headed the averages with 334 runs at 37.11 and, perhaps more important, seems to have recovered his zest for the game. The *Leytonstone Express and Independent* wrote that 'The addition to the team of A.P.Lucas not only strengthened the side from the batting point of view, but his presence has had a most satisfactory effect by encouraging the less prominent to more strenuous exertions.' Essex were nevertheless £3,850 (£230,000 today) in debt to their bankers and in grave danger of having to sell the Leyton ground and wind up the club. At a Special General Meeting on 17 October

---

84  Newspaper quotations in this chapter are mostly from the *Leytonstone Express and Independent*, which gave excellent coverage of all local cricket, including the county club.
85  *Memorial Biography of Dr W.G.Grace*, Green's contribution, p 71.

the club made one of its frequent appeals for funds and Lucas with five guineas (£300 today) was among the larger individual donors. There is no record that he was as generous again, perhaps because he felt his priority was brother Percy's family.

## 1890

In 1890 the counties established a Second-Class Counties Championship consisting of Cheshire, Derbyshire, Essex, Hampshire, Leicestershire, Somerset, Staffordshire and Warwickshire. Matches could only be considered first-class if they were played over three days, and the second-class counties were moving towards that status by regularly playing three-day games against one another and some of the first-class counties, most notably Yorkshire, Lancashire and Surrey. *Cricket* magazine considered it was in 1890 that Essex 'commenced to set their house in order with a view to a higher place on county cricket.' Their list of ten matches was their strongest to date and Lucas was able to play in all but two of them.

Contemporary references to the captaincy are few but Lucas apparently shared it with Cyril Buxton, a fine all-round sportsman who was the English rackets champion in 1888. He was the son of Edward North Buxton, chairman of the family brewing firm and an influential figure in west Essex, who had always been generous in his support of the club. Green's *Wisden* obituary noted that he 'was fond of recalling the fact that two Cambridge cricketers who threw in their fortunes with Essex – A.P.Lucas and the late C.D.Buxton – followed him at the University at intervals of ten and twenty years respectively, and, like himself, played four times against Oxford. Lucas was in the Cambridge eleven from 1875 to 1878, and Buxton from 1885 to 1888.'

After defeats by Surrey and Derbyshire and a draw with Warwickshire, Essex welcomed Yorkshire to Leyton for the first time. They dismissed the visitors for 74 and 140 and needed only 23 to win, but heavy rain meant that 'they were deprived of a match in all points of which they had shewn marked superiority.' In Lucas's next game, on an awkward wicket at Derby, a victory target of 53 was far from a formality but he took charge with a fine unbeaten 35, winning the match with a boundary.

Lucas returned to Leyton to play for Cambridge University Past and Present against the Australians. He put on 71 for the first wicket with Owen but the feature of the Cambridge innings was a brilliant 145 in 110 minutes by a cousin of the famous children's novelist Noel Streatfeild, the 20-year-old undergraduate Edward Streatfeild, who then took five for 47. Lucas chipped in with one for 5 as the Australians followed on 171 behind. They were soon 14 for two but a 276-run partnership between Harry Trott and Billy Murdoch enabled them to declare and set Cambridge 185 to win in 85 minutes. Lucas bowled 24 economical five-ball overs for only 27 runs but could not make the breakthrough. In an attempt to force the win,

Cambridge captain Sammy Woods 'very unwisely altered their order of going in, and the early batsmen playing a rash hitting game when runs were of no value, the match was soon in a critical position.' Lucas, coming in at No.6, played a typically defensive rearguard innings and, although he was eventually out for 12, he helped save the game with Cambridge on 78 for eight.

The end of the season was disappointing for Lucas and for Essex. Leicestershire and Surrey both beat Essex by fairly narrow margins which could well have been reversed if he had batted as well as he had earlier in the season. An overall record of one win, five losses and four draws represented a decline from the previous season, but only two of the defeats were heavy and the home draw against Yorkshire would certainly have been won but for the rain. The fall of Lucas's own average from 42 to 22 was due partly to his loss of form late in the season, but also to the wretched weather that affected everybody.

## *1891*

Lucas advised the committee that, because of business commitments, he would not be available for the first four county matches – more than usual, so possibly related to Percy's affairs. They formally offered the captaincy to Cyril Buxton. The young professional Herbert ('Bob') Carpenter, son of the great Robert of Cambridgeshire, opened the innings with some success so, with typical thoughtfulness and keenness to encourage young talent, Lucas returned at No.3. In Buxton's absence, Lucas captained the side against Hampshire at Leyton and 'hit freely' for 26 and 18, but after his dismissal Essex collapsed and lost by 21 runs.

Against Warwickshire at Leyton Lucas's 72 was easily the highest score in the match, and Essex won by ten wickets. It was probably in this game that Lucas took on a new role, that of wicket-keeper. Since 1888, Essex's regular keeper had been George Littlewood, a Lancashire import described by Lillywhite as 'quite among the first flight of keepers', but after the Hampshire defeat he was dropped for the rest of the season, either through loss of form or for disciplinary reasons. Lucas had kept wicket at school but there is no record of his having done so since, so it was quite a departure for the 34-year-old. He usually fielded in the outfield and had not taken a single catch in 1890, but in three matches held six catches and took a stumping. In the return game against Warwickshire he played 'a brilliant innings of 113 made without a single blemish in three hours, with chief hits of 13 fours.'

With four wins, Essex began to fulfil the promise of the previous year and, but for the Hampshire defeat, would have won the Second-Class Championship. Lucas finished the season with 315 runs at 35.00.

## 1892

*Lillywhite* commented that Essex 'can put a strong eleven in the field, and with its full strength is a formidable combination'. They must therefore have approached the 1892 season optimistically, but for them it was one of the gloomiest in an often gloomy tale. On 10 May, Cyril Buxton committed suicide while severely depressed, and the tragedy cast a pall over the whole season. Mr and Mrs Lucas were among the many who sent wreaths to the funeral. Buxton had seemed in good health and spirits at the club's AGM only a few days earlier, and was eagerly looking forward to the first two games of the season, against Surrey and Yorkshire. Essex began the Surrey game only six days after his death and the *Leytonstone Express and Independent* commented: ' ... there can be little doubt that in taking the field for the first time his absence from their ranks will be forcibly brought home to the players.' Business kept Lucas out of both games, and not surprisingly Essex lost heavily.

The committee nevertheless asked Lucas to resume the captaincy and he managed to get to Leyton in early June for Essex's next game, against Derbyshire. He contributed little with the bat but his calming influence would have been helpful to a young and inexperienced side, and they won by five wickets. The feature of the match was the first major performance by the promising 21-year-old fast bowler Charles Kortright, already a friend and admirer of Lucas, who in the first innings bowled 31 overs unchanged and took eight for 58. Wicket-keeper Littlewood was horribly out of form with the bat and perhaps with the gloves too, so Lucas became the unlucky Essex man who subjected his hands to a battering from the young man's thunderbolts. Against Warwickshire, he made a second stumping for Essex and took a catch off the promising young off-spinner Walter Mead.

Combining the captaincy with keeping wicket did not affect Lucas's batting and he shared several good partnerships with the hard-hitting amateur A.S.Johnston, but both men were absent for home defeats against Surrey and Yorkshire. 'Cover Point' suggested in the *Leytonstone Express and Independent* that Essex should ...

> content herself playing good second-class counties and by doing give the players a little encouragement. Undoubtedly the frequent losses have a depressing effect on the players and a few more wins would ... make each and all strive for the position in the first-class batch of counties. ... Essex could put much better teams in the field than she does when first-class fixtures are on ... Messrs A.P.Lucas and A.S.Johnston have only played in seven fixtures to the present and these are two really good men.

The criticisms have echoes of the 'Surrey Veteran' remark ten years earlier, but there is a great difference: Lucas was not appearing for other teams, but deliberately choosing to play only in those Essex matches he considered most important. 'Cover Point' overlooked the fact that Lucas and Johnston, a corn merchant, had to earn a living and could not play cricket whenever they felt like it.

Lucas headed the averages with 347 runs at 31.54, so will have been reasonably pleased with his own form, but not with that of his team, which won three, drew three and lost seven. Attendances were therefore very poor and the overall deficit was £2,500, about £150,000 today. In November 1892 an Extraordinary General Meeting was held at the Great Eastern Hotel, Liverpool Street. C.E.Green presided, and outlined 'the very serious position in which the club was placed'. After much debate, Green's motion that ' ... steps be forthwith taken to wind up the Essex County Cricket Club' found no seconder and 'fell to the ground'. Eventually the money was found, chiefly from Green himself and the treasurer, C.M.Tebbut.

## 1893

Speaking at the 1893 annual meeting, Green seems to have viewed the prospects for the new season more in hope than expectation, his only positive grounds for optimism being Lucas's continuing availability as captain. As usual, business commitments kept Lucas out of the first game of the season, in which Surrey beat Essex in two days and Green's pessimism seemed justified.

At Leyton against Leicestershire, Owen was due to continue deputising as captain but was taken ill, and Lucas arrived at lunch-time to find his team languishing on 102 for seven. Nos. 7 and 9, Walter Mead and Tom Russell, were already at the wicket. After lunch they added 54. Then Lucas, coming in at No.10, 'hit in his very best form' for 80 not out of 149 in 90 minutes with 11 fours. He added 66 with Mead, and 'by spirited batting Mr Lucas and Pickett added 73 in 25 minutes', so the 'rate of run-getting at the end of the Essex innings was phenomenal'. Their eventual total of 295 nevertheless seemed less than adequate when Leicestershire had cruised to 147 for two, but the visitors then lost their last eight wickets for 31 and were bowled out again for 56, giving Essex an improbable win by an innings and 61 runs.

On the scheduled last day of this match, an interview with Lucas was published as one of the *Chats on Cricket Field.* With little evidence but considerable optimism and prescience, he declared: 'I am glad, bye the bye, to think that Essex seems likely to turn the corner this year, so far as cricket is concerned.' Cricket, that great leveller, ensured that in the very next game Lucas – immediately after telling *The Cricket Field* that he had only ever had one 'pair of spectacles' – got his second, in a ten-wicket defeat by Yorkshire. Then in the return at Leicester, batting in his normal position of No.3, he made only 22 and one as Essex lost by eight wickets.

Even by Essex standards it was a roller-coaster of a season. Hampshire reached 150 for three and then 'there followed the most peculiar collapse ever seen on the County Ground'. Lucas brought back Kortright, who bowled six men in 13 balls, five of them for ducks. Mead took the other wicket and the last seven fell for none. In the Essex reply, Lucas by 'sterling cricket' made 175 in 275 minutes with eighteen fours. It was his highest score in a county match, and at that time the highest by any Essex player. He gave no chance and only a couple of strokes were even risky. He put on 111 for the fifth wicket with Henry Taberer and 155 for the ninth with Tom Russell, who had taken over as wicket-keeper and batted splendidly for 84 not out. Kortright and Mead bowled Hampshire out for 114 and Essex won by an innings and 177.

*A sterling though not first-class 175, as recorded by Joe Armour, against Hampshire at Leyton in July 1893.*

Russell told *Cricket* in 1897: 'Mr Lucas is a splendid bat. Whatever I have been able to do as a bat ... has been from watching Mr Lucas. I have once or twice been lucky enough to be in with him for a long time, and it has been an education to me.' Tom's son C.A.G. ('Jack') learned much from his father and on retirement in 1930 became coach at Westminster School. Thus a thread of mutual respect between amateurs and professionals – with rare exceptions a characteristic of Essex cricket – can be traced from H.H.Stephenson through Lucas and the Russells for sixty years.

Essex, without Lucas, then beat that season's champions, by seven wickets. Yorkshire scored only 44 and 127, and Lord Hawke declared that any county which could bowl his team out for under 50 should be playing in the first-class county championship.

The next game at Leyton was due to be the traditional first-class one between Cambridge University Past and Present and the Australians, but Cambridge failed to raise a strong enough side so Essex took over the fixture at short notice. The match was not classified as first-class, although the quality of play was higher than in many that have been. The Australians continued to play the University itself, but the Past and Present fixture was never revived.

'Whatever I have been able to do as a bat ...
has been from watching Mr Lucas.'
Tom Russell in 1897.

Essex were able to put out their strongest side, consisting of six amateurs and five professionals. The Australians batted first and were bowled out in 3¼ hours, but not before they had rattled up 250 at 77 an hour. Essex closed on 72 for two but unfortunately the second day was one of the few wet ones in a glorious summer and Essex did not complete their innings of 237 until the third morning. Lucas was caught and bowled by Hugh Trumble for 15, the first of several encounters between two cricketers who were to develop a great respect for one another. At 6 feet 4 inches Trumble was exceptionally tall for a spinner, bowling at near medium pace and giving the ball a good tweak with his long fingers.

On the rain-affected pitch, Essex bowled the tourists out for 141 in 2½ hours, but less than half an hour remained and, amid some scepticism, they emerged with rather the better of the draw. In the match, Mead bowled 73 overs unchanged and took 17 wickets for 205, a record-breaking performance recognised by a somewhat ungenerous collection of £8, presented to him by C.E.Green on the pavilion balcony. Essex were perhaps fortunate in getting the fixture at short notice, but they made the most of their opportunity and achieved a famous result that contributed to their obtaining first-class status the following season. Mead's seventeen-wicket return has been a footnote in first-class record books ever since.

Lucas and his team had their best win in their last home game, against Surrey. He won the toss and chose to bat on a 'wicket that looked well, but from the small totals made by either side on first innings, must have belied its appearance'. Essex were bowled out for 62 in 65 minutes but gained an improbable first innings lead of eight, Kortright taking eight for 29. In the second innings 'Carpenter and "Captain" Lucas made things lively by a most unexpected and meritorious stand' of 59, both batting 'confidently and well.' Lucas was eventually seventh out, having 'played brilliantly' for 58 in 130 minutes, in a match where the next highest individual score was Carpenter's 22. Surrey were dismissed for 76 and Essex won by 102 runs.

Kortright and Mead bowled unchanged throughout the match, at which there was 'a capital attendance', and it was appropriate that they and Lucas 'came in for an enthusiastic ovation at the finish of the game' – not only for their performance in that match, but throughout the season. Mead took 119 wickets and Kortright 78, both at a fraction under 16 and far ahead of Pickett with 34 at 17. Lucas scored 599 runs at 46.07, both figures double those of Russell who was next on the list. *Wisden* described Lucas in 1893 as 'a tower of strength', and the Essex annual report commented: 'Individual mention must be made of the sterling and consistent batting of Mr A.P.Lucas and the splendid bowling of Mr C.J.Kortright and Mead, who have been of immense assistance in all the county matches.' C.E.Green told *The Cricket Field*: 'All Essex men owe a debt of gratitude to A.P.Lucas, who at great inconvenience to himself played in nearly all the matches, and captained the team with great ability.'

Conditions for batting in a glorious summer were often easy and some opposing attacks weak, but Lucas seems to have batted with greater freedom than at any time in his career. Much like Trevor Bailey more than half a century later, he had a reputation as a solid defensive player, but could attack with great flair when bowling was not of the highest class and the situation demanded, most notably with his unbeaten 80 in 90 minutes when batting No.10 against Leicestershire. He was better known for his rearguard actions to save games but, in three of the four Essex wins in which he played, it was his positive batting that gave his bowlers enough runs to bowl at.

Essex had experienced an inconsistent but encouraging season. They had the rather curious record of winning once and losing once against each of the five counties they played. They lost to Hampshire, who won only one other game, yet they were the only second-class county to defeat the joint 'second-class' champions, Derbyshire, and the only team to beat both Yorkshire and Surrey. Best of all, they more than held their own with the Australians.

Reviewing Essex's season, the *Leytonstone Express and Independent,* which only a year earlier had argued that Essex should 'content herself playing good second-class counties', commented: 'Their all-round cricket was worthy of a first-class county, and it is to be hoped the fact will not be lost sight of when the next readjustment is considered at Lord's.' The fact was indeed not lost sight of: in April 1894 a meeting of the first-class captains resolved to ask MCC to regard three-day matches played by Derbyshire, Essex, Leicestershire and Warwickshire as first-class. MCC decided that second-class status should be abolished and counties were to be deemed first-class or otherwise. All four counties were granted first-class status, although it was too late for them to arrange enough matches to enter the Championship. When they did so in 1895 they were joined by Hampshire.

## *1894*

Essex had felt for some years that the club could only pay its way if it obtained first-class status, so the achievement was the cause of great rejoicing and 403 new members were elected during the season, but it proved a bitter disappointment. It was fortunate for Essex that they did not enter the Championship, because they did not win a single county match and would have finished bottom. *Lillywhite*'s comment was a masterpiece of understatement: 'Unfortunately for Essex the ill luck which has followed them with such singular pertinacity for the last three or four years did not desert them when good fortune would have been particularly useful. ... The want of another reliable bowler was sorely felt at times and the out-cricket was susceptible of improvement without a doubt.'

For Lucas the season was equally disastrous. He played in only six of the eleven matches, and only one of the last five. He scored a mere 88 runs, with an average below ten – ridiculously low for such a fine player. There is no obvious explanation for his failure, particularly by contrast with the previous year. Perhaps he suffered the loss of form that comes to all players and had little opportunity to put it right, or there was a crisis in his business affairs that affected his usually intense concentration and kept him out of the team at the end of the season. Lucas must have felt some responsibility for the team's failures, but it was only on 16 May 1895 that the committee discussed his letter 'resigning the captaincy owing to business engagements.' They accepted his resignation with regret and offered the captaincy to Hugh Owen, who had often led the side in his absence and was the obvious choice to take over. Since Essex had already played two matches, their first ever in the Championship, the committee were probably only ratifying a decision that had already been made.

*Lucas eventually played sixty first-class matches at 'dear old' Leyton, more than at any other ground. This picture was taken in 1900.*

# Chapter Eleven
## Essex cricketer, 1895-1907

No longer captain, Lucas made an important contribution to Essex's success over the next few years and, as *The Times* obituary put it, 'his method served him so well that right into middle age he kept up his form.' While with Essex, Lucas experimented with an unusually long-handled bat. Home Gordon, in a 1906 article entitled *Some Notable Cricket Bats*, succeeds in filling half a page of charming anecdotes about Lucas without mentioning the bat or his reasons for using it, on which we can only speculate. Gordon comments on Lucas's 'wonderful facility of meeting the ball with the centre of the bat' and his very fine playing of the cut stroke, so perhaps Lucas found that the bat gave him a little extra reach in making his favourite shots.

### 1895 and 1896

Lucas's plea of business commitments in 1895 was genuine enough, for he played in only four of Essex's 17 games. In the first of them, in early June, he carried on much as he had left off the previous year, bowled for nought and three by Leicestershire's Arthur Woodcock. Woodcock took 12 wickets but the feature of the match was in the first innings when Harry Pickett took ten for 32, still the best analysis by an Essex bowler, and found himself on the losing side. Tragically, Woodcock and Pickett were both to take their own lives.

Lucas next played in mid-July at Taunton. At last he returned to his old form, though not perhaps in the most testing of circumstances. By then he had dropped down to seven and he came to the crease with Essex handily placed on 358 for five, having bowled Somerset out for 246. The Somerset bowling was 'none too deadly' and Essex progressed at a steady 100 runs an hour. Carpenter and McGahey had already hit hundreds and Lucas's 135 was the third, with 18 fours and a six. Tom Russell was again 'lucky enough to be in with him for a long time', though unlucky to fall one short of being Essex's fourth centurion, which would at that time have been a record in a single innings. They added 184 for the eighth wicket, an Essex record that stood until 1936, when Jimmy Cutmore and Peter Smith put on 214 against the Indians. Essex's 692 was the highest score ever made at Taunton but it was one of cricket's shorter-lived records, for in the very next game Lancashire made a little matter of 801. Essex's winning margin of an innings and 317, however, remains their largest, and the total their highest until 1990.

Remarkably, Lucas's third outing of the season two weeks later also saw an Essex record that has never been beaten – Walter Mead's match return of 17 for 119 against Hampshire. If Essex's 1893 match against the Australians had been deemed first-class, he would have been, at that time, the only man ever to get 17 wickets in a match twice. As with Pickett's record earlier in the season, Essex lost comfortably. In the first innings Lucas top-scored with 37 and added 56 at a run a minute with Kortright. He got a duck in the second and another in Essex's next game, and missed the rest of the season.

In 1896 Lucas was able to play in only three of Essex's 14 games. The first of them was against the Australians, whom he always seems to have been keen to take on. He came in with Essex on 74 for four and was last man out, for 46 out of 166. In the second innings he was out for 16 and the Australians won comfortably by seven wickets. Lucas was run out without scoring against Warwickshire but made 42 and 56 in a big win at Derby.

*The Essex side which played the Australians at Leyton in May, 1896.*
*Standing (l to r): W.Mead, C.J.Kortright, J.W.Armour (scorer), H.Pickett,*
*T.M.Russell (wk).*
*Seated: P.A.Perrin, A.P.Lucas, H.G.P.Owen (capt), C.P.McGahey,*
*H.A.Carpenter.*
*On the step: F.G.Bull, J.F.Bawtree.*

Under Owen's leadership, Essex recovered from the disappointments of 1894, finishing eighth in the Championship in 1895 and fifth in 1896. Though Lucas appeared little in those years, his contribution was appreciated. *Wisden* stated that 'Lucas did quite sufficient to prove the loss of his side sustained in being unable to command his services more often.' Interviewed for *Chats on the Cricket Field*, Pickett declared that Essex's success owed much to the generosity of Green and the treasurer, C.M.Tebbut, and to the play of Lucas and Owen. Green, at a fund-raising dinner in his honour in December 1896, described Lucas as 'one of the most brilliant and scientific cricketers ever produced by England'.

## 1897

In 1897 Lucas was forty years old and had managed only thirteen first-class games in three years. On his first appearance of the season *The Times* commented, 'it is a pity he should be so little seen now in first-class matches,'[86] but they had their wish and he played no fewer than ten games. Though not formally listed on the Stock Exchange as a partner in Booth Bros until 1898, he was probably working with them a year earlier and thus able to get away more often.

Lucas made a sparkling start to the season with two not outs against Surrey; an 'exceptionally pretty innings' of 59 with a five and nine fours was followed by a rapid 57 but Essex could not quite force the win. He did little in the next three games but was back to his best against Hampshire when he scored 70 'in his own inimitable style' and Essex won by an innings. Against Derbyshire he came in with Essex on 29 for four and made 89, putting on a match-winning partnership of 123 with A.J.Turner, a brilliant young recruit for Essex who was born when Lucas was still up at Cambridge. Home Gordon[87] tells a rather moving tale about this partnership: 'The beautiful form of the veteran was matched by an almost marvellously close reproduction of his methods by the young Woolwich cadet. The latter was the recipient of congratulations, but on inquiry confessed that he had never, until that very day, seen Mr A.P.Lucas bat. The similarity therefore became phenomenal, but an explanation was soon found. Major Turner had been coached by his father, who was one of the ill-fated cricket team under Major Dunn, lost when the *Bokhara* went down. The parent had been an ardent admirer of the methods of Mr A.P.Lucas, and set them up as the desirable standard when teaching his son.'

In five completed innings in July Lucas scored only 68 runs, but played a useful role for the side in three games by taking over as wicket-keeper from the injured Tom Russell. In the first of the six innings he conceded 20 byes and, in the remaining five, let through 30, certainly more than Russell

---

86   Most match quotes in this chapter taken from *The Times*.
87   Gordon, *op cit.*, p 455.

would have done, but held three catches including one off Kortright who was still at his fearsome fastest.

Lucas had appeared in ten of Essex's twelve county matches but played in none of the four in August. He was still a fine batsman and is unlikely to have been dropped, so the most likely explanation is business. He may also have felt he wasn't needed: Russell had recovered from injury, Turner had made a wonderful start to his career and another promising young batsman, 22-year-old Frederick Fane, had returned from Oxford in good form.

On 7 August, before a Saturday last-day crowd of 15,000, Essex beat Lancashire at Leyton to go top of the table. The *Leytonstone Express and Independent* headlined its report, perhaps with some disbelief, as 'At the Top at Last'. Had Essex beaten Surrey the following week they would have taken the championship ahead of Lancashire and Surrey, but they lost by ten wickets inside two days. Essex nevertheless came third, a position they did not surpass for over eighty years, and their oldest player doubtless took a quiet satisfaction in the success of his adopted county. Lucas, with 386 runs at 35.09, was fourth in the Essex averages behind Turner and the 'Essex Twins', Percy Perrin and Charles McGahey.

## 1898

Essex had been transformed from a club that few counties wanted to play into one of the strongest in the country, so they arranged new home and away fixtures with Gloucestershire and Kent. Lucas, at the age of 41, played in thirteen games – more county matches than ever in his career. With 281 runs in ten innings, often on difficult pitches, he made a sound start to the season. *The Times* commented on his 62 against Warwickshire: 'As for Mr Lucas, nothing could have been better than his timing of the fine-length ball, and his mastery of the ball revived memories of his great cricket days at Uppingham and Cambridge.' He also continued to be a fine fielder: Yorkshire's first innings at Leyton ended with 'a remarkable catch by Mr Lucas at mid-on, when he held a hard drive low down with his left hand.'

One of the most remarkable games of this or any other season was at Old Trafford. Lancashire were in control for most of the match and eventually set Essex 336 to win. At that time, no side batting last in county cricket had ever scored more than 300 and won. After Owen and Carpenter made a solid start, McGahey and Perrin put on 191 for the third wicket but then Perrin and Turner were both out on 279. Lucas came in with four wickets down and 57 still needed. Lancashire sensed a chance of victory so their bowling and fielding were tight. The score advanced very slowly but Lucas's experience was invaluable. McGahey was batting brilliantly and while he was there made most of the runs, but when he was finally out for 145 with Essex still 23 short, Lucas took charge. His unbeaten 23 saw them home by four wickets to 'a brilliant victory for Essex' (*Express and Independent*) and 'an unprecedented achievement' (*Wisden*).

In Owen's absence, Lucas captained the side for the first time since 1894, against Surrey. In the second innings he put on 103 in 130 minutes with Perrin, but then had little support and was last out after 'a grand innings' of 89 with nine fours. Although Surrey also collapsed, Lucas had too few runs to play with and his side lost by five wickets.

*The Times* considered that 'Essex were at a great disadvantage' when he and Tom Russell were so affected by the 'great heat' that they could not take part in the match against Gloucestershire. Essex would have missed Lucas not only for his batting but also as reserve wicket-keeper, and they lost by an innings. Perhaps because of his indisposition, Lucas also missed the last two games of the season.

Essex dropped from third to fifth place, which *Wisden* described as 'not as good as they had hoped' and 'not quite commensurate with the merits of the eleven.' They lost four more games than in 1897, but won three more and their cricket was always entertaining, so crowds were good. Lucas with 472 runs at 29.50 was third in the Essex averages behind the 'Essex Twins', Turner having suffered a touch of 'second-season syndrome.'

## *1899*

Essex's first game was against the Australians. Essex won the toss and batted but the wicket was difficult and Lucas came in just before lunch with the score on 84 for five. Among the Australians was all-rounder Charlie McLeod, who was deaf in one ear. Though only in early middle age, Lucas also was going deaf. There followed an amusing misunderstanding that was recalled by two of the Australians, Clem Hill and Hugh Trumble.[88] McLeod was fielding at mid-on and therefore close enough to Lucas when he was not facing the bowling to talk to him. McLeod asked Trumble: 'This chap Lucas is a funny old stick. I speak to him but he won't answer.' Trumble, with his quick wit, at once saw the humour of the situation and replied, 'Oh, he's one of those stuck-up fellows who thinks no end of himself.' Later in the day, Lucas spoke to McLeod, but this time it was McLeod who did not answer. The Australians had a good laugh in the dressing-room that evening. Lucas and McLeod were brought together, explanations followed, and they became great pals.

Lucas put on 31 with his old ally Tom Russell but soon Essex were 144 for nine. He was joined by Harding Isaac Young, a gangling left-arm seamer who had been 'bought out' of the Navy by C.E.Green and was nicknamed 'Sailor'. Young had no pretensions as a batsman but made 33 in as many minutes with lusty leg-side hitting, and they added 55 for the last wicket. *The Times* commented that Lucas's 46 not out was 'the great batting of the day. ... It took a long time to get; but some of his drives along the ground

---

88    Bernard Whimpress (ed), *Clem Hill's Reminiscences*, ACS Publications, 2007. Trumble's account described in Reese, Daniel, *Was it All Cricket?*, Allen and Unwin, 1948. The two versions differ slightly but are essentially the same and I have conflated them.

were perfect, and now and again he came out perfectly on the leg side.' He scored two 4s and no fewer than six 3s, a tribute to the fitness of the 42-year-old and to the skilful placing of his strokes. Trumble bowled superbly and took eight for 79 in the first innings but later complained: 'Confound old Lucas, I can't get him out. The old beggar must be ninety, but I'm hanged if he doesn't keep improving.'[89]

Mead and Young bowled equally well to dismiss the Australians for 144, which was Essex's score when their ninth wicket went down and thus emphasised the importance of the last-wicket partnership. Essex then made exactly 144 themselves, their only significant partnership one of 93 in 110 minutes between McGahey and Turner, who were greatly assisted by uncharacteristically slovenly Australian catching. Lucas again batted at No.7 and was not out, but made only eight before running out of partners.

The Australians had all day to make 200 but were dismissed in 39.4 five-ball overs for 73. Young, with seven for 32, was unplayable, and well supported by Mead with three for 32. Hill 'fell to a magnificent catch by Lucas in the slips, the old Cantab taking the ball high above his head when running back, and falling backwards with the ball in his hand'. A crowd of thousands swarmed round the pavilion, as was usual at Leyton on such occasions, and Green gave a passionate speech from the balcony. He dragged the captain to the front but 'Mr Owen bowed, blushed and then, breaking away, dived through a doorway behind him like a rabbit into a hole'.[90] Lucas was even more averse to any fuss and was the only player not even enticed on to the balcony, preferring to slip away by the back door.

Lucas then missed six consecutive county games, presumably for business reasons. He reappeared against Warwickshire, who on a damp pitch set Essex a tantalising target of 129 in about two hours. Essex made a positive start but slipped from 52 for one to 54 for five, and Lucas batted out time for a draw.

Essex won four county games before Lucas returned but, after a heavy and unexpected defeat by Derbyshire, the committee complained because the pitch had been under-prepared. Head groundsman Ted Freeman consulted Sam Apted, the groundsman at The Oval where the pitches were excellent, but Apted's advice led to a famous misunderstanding. He told Freeman to apply a liquid mixture 'three days before the match' but the Essex man applied the mixture on each of the three days rather than just on the third day before. The pitch was ruined and even Lucas was unable to cope with it. Ironically, the visitors were Surrey who bowled Essex out for 37 in 75 minutes and won by nine wickets in two days, so the committee were even more dissatisfied.

---

89   Quoted, Sale, *op cit.*, p 2. This is only error I have found in Sale's excellent book. He suggests that Lucas frustrated Trumble in Test matches, but Trumble's Test début came six years after Lucas's last Test, so Trumble was presumably referring to an Essex game, and this is the most likely candidate.

90   Meredith, *op cit.*, p 89.

Lucas had been out of form and was unfortunate to miss two matches where Essex ran up big scores on excellent pitches and won easily. He may well have missed more but Turner, who had been in fine form, was called away on Army duty to the South African war. Lucas came back to his best with 67 in a rain-affected draw at Derby, but an unbeaten 55 against Lancashire and 39 against Gloucestershire were in vain as Essex lost both games heavily. In the final game he captained the side in Owen's absence and his declaration set Warwickshire 177 in four hours to avoid an innings defeat, but rain again washed out Essex's chance of victory. Though seldom at his best, he still scored 393 runs at just over 30.

## 1900

Green, in his speech after the Australian win, expressed the hope that 'this victory was only the forerunner of good things to come', but it was not to be. Essex's decline late in the 1899 season foreshadowed the end of an era. Only Mead continued to be a force as a bowler and the Leyton wicket became one of the blandest in the country, so Essex were seldom able to bowl sides out. Military duties meant that Turner, who played 33 games for Essex from June 1897 to July 1899, only ever played another 35. The increasingly injury-prone Owen was in decline and there seems to have been an informal arrangement whereby Lucas led the side in his absence, so his services were needed more than ever.

In 1900 Lucas must have negotiated more out-of-office time with Booth Brothers, for amazingly, at the age of 43, he played 15 first-class games – more than ever before. He began the season with his first non-Essex first-class match for a decade, for MCC against Leicestershire at Lord's. The feature of the match was a brilliant partnership between Lucas and Kingsmill Key, who came together at 47 for four and added 199 for the fifth wicket in under two hours. Lucas's 95 included four fives and two fours, and MCC won by nine wickets. This was a match played under an experimental 'boundary-net' system, in which hits over the net counted three and if the ball touched the net two were added to whatever had been run. C.F.C.Clarke, a supporter of the net system, recalled: 'It was argued that if two veterans like K.J.Key and A.P.Lucas could make their hundreds without much exertion, the scheme must be a failure.'[91] Clarke said the fault was the addition of two runs when the ball touched the net and in fact the experiment was modified, but the new version proved equally impracticable and the whole thing was abandoned.

For Essex Lucas was a straight replacement for the absent Turner, even taking his place at No.5. Though he was half Lucas's age, Turner could scarcely have done better. Against Sussex his 78 was 'dashing' and, as so often, he shared his experience batting with a young professional – in this

---

91    Bettesworth, *op cit.*, p 300. Charles Frederick Carlos Clarke (1853-1931) was a contemporary of Lucas at Surrey but preferred country house and club cricket, and was a keen amateur huntsman, actor and musician.

case Bill Reeves, who made a then career-best 56 in a partnership of 100. Against Leicestershire he was 'seen to great advantage' with 54 and against Lancashire he 'played fine cricket' for 61 in 135 minutes.

Owen missed the next three matches and Lucas took over as captain. In a remarkable game against Yorkshire, Essex conceded a lead of 20 and collapsed to 43 for eight. Mead hit out 'recklessly but successfully' for 46 and Lucas kept up an end for 30 not out in a partnership of 77, but after a shaky start Yorkshire won by six wickets. Lucas then put Sussex in on a difficult wicket and they were bowled out for 108 but Essex did not find things much easier and Lucas's 44 was the highest score of the match. At that point in the season he had scored 422 runs in seven completed innings. His declaration on 160 for seven was bold and Mead reduced Sussex to 14 for five, but they managed eventually to set a target of 69 in 55 minutes. Essex themselves collapsed to 31 for five and Lucas's dismissal for two brought his golden run to an end.

Loss of form, rain and flat Leyton wickets meant that Essex won no game after early June. It was their worst run since entering the Championship, and the resulting position of tenth was their lowest. Lucas scored only one fifty in the last six matches but still finished fourth in the Essex averages with 531 runs at 27.94.

## 1901

The season began with a win over Sussex which featured a partnership of 163 between McGahey (125) and Lucas (83). *The Times* was effusive:

> In his great days at Cambridge and Uppingham, Mr A.P.Lucas never played more brilliant cricket than he did at the Lyttelton Ground, Leyton, yesterday, when with Mr McGahey he turned a losing game into one that now spells success. ... Yesterday his method of dealing with a short ball was perfect; and in dealing with the good-length bowling on the hard wicket his straight bat and his power of striking were inimitable. He was handicapped through a strain in his knee, which made it necessary to have a man to run for him; but his innings of two hours was perfection itself. ... Mr McGahey played brilliant cricket, although in point of style his batting did not compare with that of Mr Lucas.

In June Owen aggravated his leg injury so Lucas took over the captaincy when he was absent. Against Lancashire at Leyton the feature of the first day was 75 from Lucas, 'whose off driving and cutting were worthy of his best days.' Lancashire's John Broughton, in his first-class debut at the relatively advanced age of 28, batted well but became nervous when approaching his hundred, and it was probably with some reluctance that Lucas caught him at point when he was on 99. Carpenter, in his benefit match, made 119 but disappointing gates meant that he received only £180, and it was no coincidence that the following year this cricketer 'of irreproachable conduct' became embroiled in a bruising dispute over winter wages with the committee, which included Lucas. The game petered out as one of seven draws out of that season's eleven games at Leyton.

The dreary cricket contributed to the rapidly declining attendances and, in a discussion on the preparation of wickets there, the 1902 *Wisden* reported that:

> Both Mr C.E.Green and Mr A.P.Lucas, two of the most influential gentlemen connected with Essex cricket, made no secret of their opinion that a great mistake has been made in having the wickets prepared in the modern manner.

Given their influence, it seems strange that the Leyton ground retained its reputation as a featherbed until Essex left it in 1933.

In mid-July Lucas was 21st in the national averages with 499 runs at 41.58. After that his batting rather fell away but Owen suffered a recurrence of his leg strain and Lucas again took over as captain. Against Middlesex, Lucas declared as soon as Turner was out after 'a fine display of hard hitting' for 111, and his timing was right as Essex won by 92 runs with 20 minutes to spare. Lucas then made his first appearance at the Canterbury Festival since 1877. He hit well for 36 and added 58 in half an hour with Reeves before falling to a brilliant one-handed catch at point. He again had to decide when to declare and set a conservative 298 in three hours, but his caution was justified as Kent had no trouble in reaching 177 for three.

In a match that contrasted starkly with most at Leyton that year, Lucas captained Essex to what remains their most disastrous batting performance, just as he had done with Surrey more than twenty years earlier. Against Yorkshire he won the toss and elected to bat after rain had delayed the start, but soon found himself coming to the wicket with Essex four wickets down for one run. In a situation crying out for a captain's innings drawing on all his defensive experience, 'Mr Lucas paid the penalty for attempting a short run at a critical stage.' Perhaps trying to farm the strike, he was run out for three. Essex were bowled out for 30 in barely an hour but Yorkshire made only 104. It owed much to fine batting by Tom Taylor, an Uppingham man of a later generation, whose 44 was the only individual score over 12 in the match. A miserable day for Lucas was completed when his dismissal for a duck brought the first day's play to a close with Essex on 15 for six. Next day, Essex were soon all out for 41 to give Yorkshire a remarkable win by an innings and 33 runs, Hirst taking 12 for 29 and Rhodes six for 37. Essex had a debutant who was twice bowled by Hirst for ducks and did not bowl, but Johnny Douglas did go on to enjoy better days.

With only four wins in 21 completed matches, Essex again finished tenth. Lucas was able to play in 15 of them and scored 742 runs at 37.10. He made six fifties and held eleven catches, both his best in first-class cricket since 1883. By contrast with Owen, newspapers have only one mention of an injury to Lucas, and even then he played in the next match. It seems therefore that he was remarkably fit for his age, and that his absences were for business reasons.

## *1902*

At the start of the season, Lucas was aged 45 and Owen 43. Owen played in six of Essex's first eight games but it was clear he was a spent force. He scored only 39 runs in seven innings and was almost immobile in the field. He believed that a captain should play in all the matches and commented:

> I don't think myself good enough or sound enough to do this. I find that I cannot stand the strain of playing every day throughout the summer – my leg always goes after about three weeks.[92]

Lucas had deputised for Owen since resigning the captaincy in 1895 and now officially shared it with him. Though physically far fitter than Owen, he was growing increasingly deaf so it was hardly a forward-looking decision, and it was not surprising that Essex dropped to thirteenth, with only two wins.

*Lucas wielding his experimental long-handled bat for the benefit of the photographer in about 1902. The handle appears to be about 15 in long, so presumably its blade was reduced to 23 in.*

Lucas played only three games before mid-July and, in a notoriously rain-sodden summer, all three were affected by weather. At Leyton against Kent, Essex enjoyed the best of the conditions and won by an innings in two days. Unusually, their fielding was described as very good and Lucas himself held two catches, so it may be that he was able to inspire a greater degree of athleticism than the lumbering Owen.

Owen made his final appearance for Essex on 14 July and Lucas returned to the side on the 21st, at Leicester. With Carpenter disaffected and out of form, Essex had been struggling to find an opening partner for Fane and Lucas took on the role, making only 26 but playing 'in splendid style'. Apart from this, the only away games he played were at The Oval and Canterbury. He was normally happy to travel, so perhaps there was some reason why he needed to be within easy access of his office.

---

92    *Essex Chronicle*, 1 May 1903.

On 28 July the Australians came to Leyton, fresh from Old Trafford and the famous three-run win that brought back memories of the Ashes Test twenty years before. Lucas won the toss, and on a benign wicket the tourists found bowling altogether more difficult than they had two days earlier. In front of a large and enthusiastic crowd Essex made 345, and despite Victor Trumper's fine 109 in 90 minutes, the visitors were dismissed for 232. Trumble twice bowled Lucas but not before the veteran had scored 26 and 50 'in classic style'. Lucas declared five minutes after lunch and set the Australians 297 to win in 165 minutes. After the Leyton crowd were treated to another Trumper century, the match ended in a draw with the visitors on 253 for six.

Two weeks later Lucas had the opportunity for a final tilt at the Australians when he was invited to captain MCC against them at Lord's. Most of the counties were playing, so apart from Ranjitsinhji, who had temporarily fallen out with Sussex, the MCC team was rather weak. The game came immediately after England's thrilling one-wicket victory at The Oval, so there was a disappointing lack of atmosphere. Lucas batted well for 27 in the first innings but Trumble had 'the old beggar' caught at the wicket for 11 in the second, and the Australians won by an innings.

Lucas had enjoyed the festival atmosphere at Canterbury and returned at the earliest possible opportunity. Essex were caught on a drying wicket that was expected to be difficult, but 'Mr Lucas played with all his usual elegance and power' for 42 out of 81 added in an hour with Fane. Further rain ruined the game and 'neither captain took it seriously. Mr Mason changed his batting order and Mr Lucas tried some quite unusual bowlers.'

Against Derbyshire Lucas was dropped on 0 and in the fifties but otherwise batted 'in perfect style'. He 'made most of his runs behind the wicket, his placing on both sides being admirable'. He was last out for 103, the eighth and final century of his first-class career, although he had scored three for Essex pre-first-class. Essex took a first innings lead of 62 but free hitting by the Derbyshire tail enabled them to set a target of 160 and they won an exciting game by 15 runs.

Lucas's final game as Essex captain was at Leyton against Leicestershire. Though he made only three and 12, it was a memorable swansong. After conceding a first innings lead of 172, Essex lost their second wicket shortly before the close of the second day. Mead went in as nightwatchman and in 90 minutes he made 119, the only century of his career. According to E.H.D.Sewell, whose anecdotes sometimes seem more colourful than reliable, it might never have happened but for him.[93] The secretary, O.R.Borradaile, called out to Sewell to tell Sailor Young to go in but Young 'hadn't spent valuable years in the Royal Navy for nothing ... and so was conveniently not on deck'. Mead was, so Sewell said: 'Get 'em on, Walter, Borry says you've to go in if a wicket falls.' Mead made 'almost every stroke in the good books, and several that, if he'd been bowling, he'd have liked

---

93      Sewell, E.H.D. *Well Hit! Sir*, Stanley Paul, 1946, p 89.

t'other fellow to try'. More big hitting enabled Lucas to declare on 437 for eight and set Leicestershire 266 to win in just under three hours. They responded in kind and had reached 155 for four when rain brought a disappointing but appropriate end to Essex's last game in this soggiest of summers.

In nine matches for Essex, Lucas scored 340 runs at 26.15 and *Wisden* commented: 'Lucas batted with a skill that, considering his connection with first-class cricket began in 1874, was nothing less than astonishing.' At the end of the season he stood down as captain for the third and final time.

## 1903 to 1907

In 1903 Charles Kortright took over as captain and immediately injected more youthful verve into the side, especially in its fielding. Young players such as Rev Frank Gillingham were coming through and at first Lucas wasn't needed, but Gillingham had to fit his cricket round his duties as curate at Leyton parish church so, at the beginning of June, Lucas came in to cover him. Against Nottinghamshire he made 49, and against Sussex his resolute 47 not out in 1¾ hours was crucial, for although the pitch appeared to play well, Essex lost four wickets in knocking off 51. *The Times* reported that 'the strength of his back play showed that his strong defence remains unimpaired', but at the age of 46 his years finally began to catch up with him: in a further eleven innings he scored only 65 runs, and he finished the season with three ducks and an average of 12.42.

A new direction for Lucas's sporting interests is suggested by his appearance at Lord's for Cricket Golfers against Golf Cricketers, a rather eccentric match that was played in the years 1903 to 1905. He was bowled for 13 by Herman de Zoete, a stockbroker and fine amateur golfer who had played two games for Essex in 1897. Bunny's cousin Percy Montagu Lucas, father of 'Laddie', was twice Norfolk amateur champion and co-founder of Prince's Golf Club in 1904, so may have introduced him to the game.

In August 1904 Essex recalled Lucas to play in the Canterbury Week. Remarkably, he may well have kept wicket, for the *Chelmsford Chronicle* said that he replaced Tom Russell in the side, and he held three catches in the Kent first innings. He then 'signalised his reappearance in county cricket by an admirable display of sound and stylish batting'; he made 44 and with Turner added 67 in 70 minutes when Essex were in danger of following on. Sadly, the fairy tale didn't last: he made a duck in the second innings and another against Lancashire on the flattest of wickets at Leyton.

In 1905 and 1906 Lucas turned out for MCC against Cambridge University. In the 1906 game he made 34 and 33, opening with his Essex colleague Frederick Fane. *The Times* commented: 'Mr Lucas, from the point of view of the actual strokes that he makes, plays almost as well as he played 25 years ago. The bat is held as straight as ever, and the back play in particular is as sound as when he first made his name.' Cambridge's failure to set a field to him gives a clue to his methods: 'Mr Lucas made a number of strokes which an extra mid-off must have prevented, and brought off this favourite stroke of his a good many times without let or hindrance.'

Then, three years after his previous appearance for Essex, he assisted them twice more, at Leyton in August 1907. In his final championship game, against Lancashire, he scored 49 in 80 minutes and shared in a seventh wicket partnership of 118 with Sam Meston, who was born two months after the Ashes Test of 1882. *The Times* commented: 'The present is Mr Lucas's 34th season of first-class cricket and he is still able to hold his own.' He had in fact missed the 1885 and 1886 seasons through illness, but it was still a remarkable achievement: only 14 players in English first-class cricket have surpassed his career span of 34 years.

Perhaps encouraged by this performance, he played in the next game against the South Africans. He held one catch but when the tourists were nine wickets down he dropped an easy chance from Gordon White and they added a further 58 runs. He was then bowled for two ducks, in the first innings round his legs by Reggie Schwarz without playing a stroke, and in the second by a good length ball from White. Tragically, both young men died in the last month of World War I, and so the veteran outlived them both. Evidently Lucas decided it really was time to call it a day, for this was his last first-class appearance. It was an ignominious end to a distinguished career, but he had nothing to be ashamed of. Against the counties in 1907, the South African slow bowlers with their then new-fangled leg-breaks and googlies deceived many younger men than Lucas. And he was aged 50 years and 178 days, which made him the only cricketer to play for Essex when aged over 50 except in the 1920s, when careers were artificially prolonged because of the losses caused by the war.

☆ ☆ ☆ ☆ ☆

Lucas brought his gentle sense of humour to Essex. In the remarkable game against Lancashire in 1898, Owen had already tried six bowlers in an attempt to break a big partnership between Johnny Tyldesley and Frank Sugg:

> 'I say, Bunny,' Owen asked, 'what *shall* we do?' Lucas replied without any hesitation, 'Put on the worst bowler you've got,' whereupon Owen replied with equal promptitude, 'Well then, you go on next over!'[94]

Immediately Sugg scored two fours and a single, but off the first ball of Lucas's second over he pulled a full toss straight to McGahey at deep square leg. Alexander Eccles hit the next two balls for four and Owen decided that the experiment had gone on long enough, but it had served its purpose. Lancashire collapsed from 206 for two to 254 all out, and Essex

---

94    Story told by O.R.Borradaile in his *Chats on the Cricket Field* interview with W.A.Bettesworth, 1910.

went on to win the match. Although Lucas had bowled a lot in his youth, it was the only first-class wicket he took for Essex, yet it was a vital one and afterwards he often asked Owen: 'If you don't put your best bowlers on, how can you expect to get sides out?' Lucas led Essex into the County Championship and Owen took them closer to winning it than any captain before Keith Fletcher in 1979. Such banter perhaps explains why Lucas enjoyed playing for Essex so much, and helped to bring that sense of fun which characterised the best of the county's cricket in the twentieth century.

# Chapter Twelve
## Essex committee man, 1890-1912

In 1890 Lucas was elected to the Essex committee in place of George Alfred Sedgwick, who died suddenly in the autumn of 1889. Sedgwick was a solicitor who had put forward detailed proposals for a scheme to solve the club's financial problems by forming it into a limited company with a capital of £15,000 in £5 shares – 'demutualising', we would call it today.[95] The committee recommended the plan to the members, who gave it their approval, but after Sedgwick's death nobody else was keen enough to carry the scheme forward, although no other county considered such a radical move until a century later.

Lucas's election was probably an *ex-officio* courtesy in recognition of his position as captain, but it was one he could have done without. In three years he did not attend a single committee meeting, even though they were usually held at the offices of C.E.Green's shipping company, within easy walking distance of his own. Earlier at Surrey and later in his time at Essex he seems to have been a fairly conscientious committee member, so the most likely explanation is pressure of business, and perhaps pressure of the captaincy. Not unreasonably, he then offered his resignation but the secretary was instructed to write and ask him to reconsider. He did reconsider and started to attend committee meetings, though never on a regular basis.

Lucas in his later years, as an Essex committee man.

Amateur cricketers playing alongside professionals respected their cricketing skills but the amateur committee managed them in a master-servant relationship, which sometimes created a tension in individuals who were fulfilling both roles. Percy Perrin 'preferred not to be on the committee as he was still playing for the county team',[96] but Lucas and others sought to reconcile the two roles. An intriguing episode from 1902 indicates where his sympathies lay.

---

95    This chapter based on ECCC minutes, 1886-1913.
96    ECCC minutes, 26 February 1920.

On 5 June, after the first day's play of a match against Warwickshire, there was a 'Special Committee Meeting'. It was held in the pavilion rather than the usual venue, Green's offices. The only men present were Owen, the club captain; Lucas, the captain on the day; O.R.Borradaile, the secretary; and George Gadsdon, who chaired the meeting. Gadsdon, a retired coach and saddle ironmonger from Ilford, was quite an active member of the committee from 1901 to 1906. The sole business was to pass a motion, proposed by Owen and seconded by Lucas, that 'the Centre Gate of the Pavilion be used by both Amateurs and Professionals.'[97]

At the next committee meeting Green signed the minute but endorsed it 'not agreeing' – the only time he made such an addition. Although the minutes have no record that the decision was ever formally rescinded, Green evidently got his own way as usual, for in 1999 the Waltham Forest Oral History Workshop recorded fascinating recollections of Essex's last years with Leyton as its headquarters, and several interviewees recalled that the separate gates were still being used when Essex left there in 1933.

*Servants do not come and go through the front door.*
*Professionals continued to use a separate gate, just out of camera to the left,*
*until Essex left Leyton in 1933.*

This may have had its roots in a more public event at Leyton three years earlier when, by coincidence or otherwise, the opponents were Warwickshire. They were fielding an all-professional side and the committee entrusted the captaincy to Edwin Diver, a former amateur who had a track record of minor insubordination. Some of the professionals were permitted to use the amateurs' dressing-room, but Diver was told that

---

97    Generous Use of Capitals as in the original.

*A Special Committee Meeting was held in the Pavilion on the 5 June 1902.*

*Members Present ?./ Gadsden (Chairman) H.G. Owen, A.P. Lucas, and J.P. Bonadaile (Sec)*

*The following Resolution was proposed by Mr H.G. Owen and Seconded by Mr A.P.Lucas*

*"That for the future the Centre Gate of the Pavilion be used by both Amateurs and Professionals*

*(Carried)*

*This terminated the business*

*C.E. Green*
*not agreeing*

Minutes of the special committee meeting at which Lucas and others decided
that amateurs and professionals should use the same gate onto the field of play.
Note, though, C.E.Green's signed comment, not agreeing, at the end.

they must walk an extra thirty yards to come through the professionals' gate, which aroused great resentment. He arranged for one batsman to go through each gate and when it was Warwickshire's turn to field he marched them through the professionals' gate, along the boundary to the amateurs' gate and thence onto the field. These antics amused Essex's East End crowd but not their West End secretary, who made a formal complaint.[98] Lucas,

---

98    Account of the match on Cricinfo website.

who captained Essex in that match, had twice played alongside Diver for the Gentlemen, and the episode may have stuck in his mind.

And yet, on an issue of far greater importance, Lucas apparently followed the committee's line when it came into dispute with two of Essex's most respected professionals, Bob Carpenter and Walter Mead. Though conducted separately, with Carpenter in 1902 and Mead in 1903, the two disputes had very similar causes. Both were deeply disappointed with the proceeds of their benefits, which would have been nowhere near enough to ensure any sort of financial security. Carpenter received only £180 and Mead a mere £137, the lowest ever recorded for an Essex professional. The equivalents in 2010 would be no more than £10,500 and £8,000. Both had financial concerns about their families and wrote threatening to resign if they were not given an increase in their winter pay. Both were unceremoniously dropped from the side, until eventually they had to give in and write grovelling letters before they were reinstated. It cannot have enhanced their sense of fair

*C.E.Green, shipowner and cricket patron, whose wide interests included fox-hunting. He was an autocratic Master of the Essex Foxhounds, and sometimes treated professional cricketers in a similar way.*

treatment that, in April 1903, their former captain and so-called amateur, Hugh Owen, received a cheque for 200 guineas and various other gifts, albeit by special subscription. Nor when Green told a special meeting, called to discuss the club's debt of £1,500 and its possible winding up: 'If membership continues to fall off and the professionals continue to take this grasping and unpatriotic attitude, what point is there in carrying on?'

These were desperately unhappy episodes from which neither side emerged with any great credit. The editor of *Wisden*, Sydney Pardon, commented: 'One cannot help thinking that with a little tact and diplomacy the whole thing might have been got over when it first presented itself.' Both were fine players at the peak of their powers, but scarcely indispensable, and the committee were right to consider that they were being given an ultimatum. They, in turn, failed to recognise the legitimate grievances of loyal servants in a precarious profession, and forced them into a humiliating climb-down. Essex were in grave financial difficulties, but it would have cost only £20 to grant the requests of Carpenter and Mead, and the club lost far more than that when the poor results of a weakened side led to declining attendances and a further loss of income.

The minutes do not record individual views, so we do not know exactly what Lucas thought of all this. He did not attend all the meetings that discussed the disputes, although he was present on 4 November 1903 when Mead's demand was unanimously rejected, and on 11 May 1906 when an urgent meeting, called solely to discuss the reinstatement of Mead, agreed unanimously to do so. The curious episode of the professionals and the centre gate shows that Lucas had some sympathy with the pros, but perhaps did not feel sufficiently strongly to offer his own resignation over the treatment of Mead and Carpenter, and preferred to avoid a direct confrontation with his irascible old friend Green to support them.

Lucas remained on the committee after retiring as a player, although in 1908 he missed several important meetings that discussed the club's latest financial crisis, brought about when the bank demanded an immediate reduction of the club's debts and threatened to foreclose on one of two mortgages on the County Ground. He therefore resigned but, as in 1893, was persuaded to reconsider. He was getting increasingly deaf and seems to have adopted the eminently sensible policy of attending committee meetings only when he had something to contribute.

Before the 1910 season, Charles McGahey offered his resignation as captain. The committed discussed the matter at some length, and Lucas proposed that the post be offered to Rev Frank Gillingham, which was perhaps a case of special pleading by one churchman for another. Gillingham was a fine batsman, but had to fit his cricket round his clerical duties, and did not play often enough to be a realistic choice. Lucas's motion was seconded by Guy Gilbey, a hunting chum of Green's, but was defeated.[99] Eventually, McGahey was persuaded to soldier on but after another disappointing season there was general agreement that he should stand down.

Lucas then had a significant role in one of the most mysterious and controversial episodes in Essex's history. The background was the Extraordinary General Meeting of 10 November 1908, when Green reported on the bank's threatened foreclosure and announced that 'a gentleman who was a sportsman in the best sense of the word had agreed to take up the second mortgage – Mr. J.H.Douglas, father of one of the club's best cricketers.' As the result of a committee motion in 1909, seconded by Lucas, Douglas also joined the committee, which put him in a powerful position. The suspicion is that he exercised it in order to gain the captaincy for his son Johnny, but the matter may not have been as simple as that.

The captaincy had usually passed to the most senior amateur, and so the obvious candidate to succeed McGahey as Essex captain was his 'twin', Perrin. He was still a fine batsman and a knowledgeable and thoughtful

---

99    Gilbey was a member of the famous gin-distilling family. His father, Sir Walter, was the patron of the Rickling Green club that in 1882 famously conceded 920 runs to the Orleans Club, and his brother Arthur was in that Rickling side. Another brother, Tresham Gilbey, was founder and editor of *Baily's Hunting Directory*, and joint author of *The Essex Foxhounds*, published in 1896.

cricketer, but the committee seem not even to have considered him. Perrin was perhaps too taciturn to be a leader, and certainly a notoriously poor fielder who would not have been in a position to chastise the side for their continuing shortcomings in the field. Their first choice was not Johnny Douglas but Charles Kortright. He had resigned the captaincy eight years earlier because he felt he was no longer worth his place in the first team, for which he had not played since 1907, although in 1910 he enjoyed some success as captain of the Second Eleven. At a meeting on 21 February 1911, not attended by Lucas, Green proposed a motion that 'Mr C.J.Kortright be asked to consider whether he would act as Captain for 1911.' Kortright was present at the meeting and did not dismiss the proposal out of hand, but eventually declined.

At the next meeting, on 28 March, Lucas proposed a motion, seconded by Kortright, that Douglas be asked to act as captain. The minutes record nothing of the debate that led to the decision and the full truth may never be known, but it seems likely that a deal was fixed behind the scenes. Green still ruled the roost and perhaps recognised kindred spirits in both Douglases, while Kortright as captain had shown real confidence in the young man before he had done much to justify it. Lucas could well have put the motion on Green's behalf, but he was a man of great integrity and is unlikely to have done so unless he agreed with it: he had seconded old Douglas's election to the committee, and probably was a supporter of the two Douglases.

A month later, Lucas became a leading figure in opposing a change to the no-ball law put forward by MCC.[100] In 1910 there had been several instances of batsmen being given run out off a no-ball where, if the delivery had been legitimate, they would have been stumped. MCC proposed to solve the problem by having all no-balls declared dead at the moment of delivery, but Lucas, Green, Douglas and six other leading amateurs wrote to *The Times* arguing that 'this old-established and unique feature of cricket should not be abolished'. At a Special General Meeting following the AGM on 3 May, Lucas proposed an amendment that the law should be left as it was, with the addition to Law 16 of the words, 'He shall not be given "run-out" in any circumstances under which – had the ball not been a no-ball – he would have been given out stumped under Law 23.' After some discussion, the amendment and the original motion were withdrawn, and it was agreed that MCC would remind umpires that 'a batsman cannot be stumped from a no-ball'. Lucas and his allies rightly claimed that the new proposals would have made 'a drastic alteration … in the conduct and playing of the game', so their victory represents a small but significant milestone in the history of cricket.

In April 1912 Lucas accepted nomination to serve for a further three years but after a wretchedly wet season, Green, who had carried the club for thirty years, finally implemented his threat to resign as chairman and from

---

100    *The Times,* 29 April, 4 May, 12 May 1911.

the committee. The county had won only one game and finished in their then worst ever position of fifteenth of sixteen in the Championship, but that was not the reason he gave to the press in an open letter:

> I am bitterly disappointed at the lack of interest and support of the club … even among the players, and I am heartily sick of the whole thing. As an old cricketer, I am entirely out of sympathy with the way county cricket is now played, and it has become so entirely a money-making business concern that the true interest of cricket as a sport and a game is fast disappearing.

The committee was thrown into turmoil and, at a special meeting on 12 November, where Lucas was present for the first time in over a year, they decided to call a Special General Meeting for 3 December. The room at the meeting was crowded and a Mr A.Draper seemed to speak for many when he accused the committee of being un-businesslike and added: 'They tried to do their best but there will have to be changes.'

Changes there certainly were. Lucas resigned on 19 December 1912, as did Kortright, Arthur Edwards, C.E.Ridley, Guy Gilbey and four others – more than half of the committee, and the biggest clearout the club ever experienced. Lucas's resignation letter is not recorded in the minutes but he would perhaps have agreed with Gilbey who 'had no time to attend and did not approve of the way in which county cricket was being played'. Lucas was never as vocal as Green, but probably shared his views and was not sorry to stand down. The committee minutes recorded the usual expressions of regret and 'hearty vote of thanks to these gentlemen for their invaluable services', and 'hoped that whenever they were at Leyton they would make use of the committee room and balcony'.

In March 1914 the committee asked Lucas and four other longstanding committee members to accept nomination to the AGM as vice-presidents. The five men wrote to say they would have pleasure in being nominated, and were duly elected. Only Lucas had played first-class cricket, so clearly it was his contribution as a committee member that was being recognised, but in 1924 the annual report recorded with regret the death of 'one of the greatest Essex cricketers'.

# Chapter Thirteen
## Bunny, Korty and Fryerning, 1885-1923

For twenty years Lucas was a churchwarden at St. Mary's church in the pleasant village of Fryerning, south-west of Chelmsford, and when he died he was buried in the churchyard there. A cricket-pitch's length away lies another great Essex amateur, Charles Jesse Kortright (1871-1952), known as Korty. Born into the leading family of Fryerning, which owned most of the village, he became the fastest bowler of his generation, and perhaps of all time.

Kortright was already a keen cricketer when in 1885, after an outbreak of diphtheria at Brentwood School, he moved to Tonbridge. There his housemaster was Rev Arthur Lucas, who in the same year helped officiate at Bunny's wedding. Arthur soon introduced him to his famous cousin, who thrilled the young man with tales of his Australian tour in 1878/79.[101] Lucas was at first Korty's hero and later his captain, team-mate, friend and neighbour. When he was aged only seventeen, Essex invited Korty to appear at Leyton for Eleven of Public Schools v Parsees. Over the next three years he played the occasional game for Essex but it was only in 1892 that he first came into his own, possibly encouraged by Lucas when he resumed the captaincy. Kortright played ten games and headed the Essex bowling averages with 53 wickets at below 13, including three eight-wicket hauls.

Korty's father had arranged for him to work at the Mackeson family brewery in Hythe, so his name was therefore linked with Kent, a first-class county. The *Leytonstone Express and Independent* reported that ' … poor old Essex is to lose the trundling services of Kortright who, it is rumoured, is qualifying for the Hop County the next season.' Perhaps dissuaded by his hero and friend Lucas, he stayed with the county of his birth and the hot summer of 1893 provided ideal conditions for him. *Lillywhite* commented on 'the marked advance of Mr C.J.Kortright, who judging by his success in the most important matches was not far removed from the best bowler in the year.' For Essex he took 61 wickets at 15.55 and, along with Lucas and Walter Mead, played a vital role in the club's achievement of first-class status and subsequent success.

In July 1898 Kortright was involved with W.G.Grace in two magnificent – though controversial – matches, in which Lucas also had a part to play. In the first match Kortright and Grace were opponents for Essex and Gloucestershire, and in the second team-mates for the Gentlemen. Gloucestershire were one of the original nine counties and had not deigned

---

101    Meredith, *op cit.*, p 16.

to play the east London upstarts, but in the previous two years Essex had finished ahead of them in the Championship. They could postpone the confrontation no longer and a crowd of nearly 10,000 was eager to see the match. Ill-feeling between the two sides began on the first morning, when Grace successfully claimed to have caught Perrin though he clearly took it on the half-volley; even Grace's team-mate Gilbert Jessop, another great cricketer of the Golden Age, was convinced that it was not out. Essex were all out for 128, and the *Leytonstone Express and Independent* reported: 'The best innings on the side was decidedly the 31 of Lucas, who is batting as well as ever this year. He alone played Grace with the confidence born of experience, and his innings contained many capital strokes.' A fine innings of 126 by Grace gave Gloucestershire a first-innings lead of 103 but Essex fought back well in their second innings.

When Lucas came to the wicket, Essex were 180 for four; but the dubious umpiring continued and he saw Turner and Russell both out to contentious decisions. Then, when going well on 22, Lucas was given out caught at the wicket from a ball that brushed his shirt. He was outraged and as he returned to the pavilion cried out to the angry crowd: 'Cheats never prosper.' He was mild-mannered by temperament and exemplified the gentlemanly public school spirit of cricket at its best, but it was not unknown for him to show dissent. In a Rovers match in 1877, 'Lucas led off for the defence but Stephenson [as umpire] soon blighted Bunny's prospects by giving him out "when I was not within a yard of the ball!!"' And in a curious incident in 1893, when he was playing a club match for Chelmsford, he had scored 118 when a fielder claimed a boundary catch which 'was so doubtful that he appealed against it but the umpire ruled against him.'[102] It was nevertheless very unusual, which suggests that the decision was exceptionally poor, and that tensions in the game were very high.

Essex were able to set Gloucestershire only 148 to win, but Kortright was already furious at the course of events and clean bowled Board and Troup in his first over. Near the end of the day, Grace bullied umpire George Burton into reversing a decision to give him out and the whole Essex team was furious, none more so than Kortright. He demanded the ball and produced an over of short-pitched bowling that was uniquely fierce even by his standards, leaving the Doctor black and blue. One ball produced a very sharp chance which McGahey missed, and as they walked off the field the ever combative Korty expressed his displeasure. Overhearing the exchange, Grace did little to calm the atmosphere: 'Cheats never prosper,' he observed.

On the last day they returned to the fray. Kortright was convinced that he had dismissed Grace, first lbw, then caught at the wicket, but again the great man intimidated Burton into turning down the appeals. The increasingly angry bowler's third ball sent the middle stump flying out of

---

102    *Essex Chronicle*, 26 May 1893.

the ground and knocked back the leg stump. 'Surely you're not going, Doc,' smiled Kortright, 'there's still one stump standing.' It was a brave remark from a young man who was born in 1871, the year that saw some of Grace's greatest triumphs, and the Champion declared that he had never been so insulted in his life. Jessop was still batting and wrote later: 'The sense of ill feeling brooding over the game made the idea of losing the match after all that had gone on before supremely distasteful.' More intense cricket included Korty breaking Edward Wright's toe with a ball that also had him lbw, and Mead hitting the stumps with a ball that did not dislodge the bail. Finally, Jessop drove Kortright for four to see his side home by one wicket. After the game, Essex's captain, the normally amiable Hugh Owen, commented publicly: 'We can take a beating in good spirit when we are fairly beaten, but we have not been fairly beaten in this match.'

Few matches can have done more to dispel the myth of the Golden Age amateur playing for the game and not the result, yet less than two weeks later Grace and Kortright shared a scene that no film-maker seeking to illustrate the myth would have dared to script. MCC had arranged for the opening day of the Gentlemen *v* Players match to coincide with

*The Gentlemen's side which lost to the Players in W.G.'s 'fiftieth birthday match'*
*at Lord's in 1898.*
*Standing (l to r): C.J.Kortright, J.R.Mason, A.C.MacLaren, J.A.Dixon,*
*W.A.J.West (umpire).*
*Seated: S.M.J.Woods, A.E.Stoddart, W.G.Grace (capt), C.L.Townsend,*
*F.S.Jackson.*
*On the ground: E.G.Wynyard, G.MacGregor (wk).*

celebrations of Grace's fiftieth birthday, but Kortright was still so furious about the events at Leyton that initially he declined the invitation to play. Appropriately, the peacemaker was Lucas who, far from bearing a grudge, demonstrated his Christian faith in action by persuading his young friend to turn out. Nevertheless the feud continued on the field and at first they refused to speak to one another, even when Grace threw the ball to Korty to bowl the first over. Kortright's bowling was fast and furious in every sense of the phrase and eventually Grace made the first move, asking Korty whether he was fit to continue bowling in the exceptionally hot weather, and normal relations were resumed.

Set 296 to win on the final afternoon, the Gentlemen had collapsed to 80 for nine when, at 5.40, Korty joined Grace, who encouraged him to play his usual game. Korty batted very responsibly and top-scored with 46, but when going for the four that would have given him his 50, was caught off Lockwood's cleverly disguised slower ball, the third of the last over. The Gentlemen had lost, but he and Grace linked arms to leave the ground to the cheers of the crowd, who would not disperse until their amateur heroes had appeared on the balcony to acknowledge the applause.

It may well have been Lucas who encouraged Kortright to return to the side after missing the whole of the 1899 season through injury, and in 1903 to succeed him in the captaincy. Ironically, it was on Lucas's proposal that the committee unanimously invited Frederick Fane, an even more reluctant captain than Lucas himself, to take over when Kortright stood down after just one year.

\* \* \* \* \*

In 1887, having determined to qualify by residence for Essex, Lucas moved with his wife to Westfield, Broomfield Road, Chelmsford. He rented the house from another Uppingham man, a fellow member of the Rovers, C.E.Ridley, who lived nearby at The Elms. A member of the noted Essex brewing family, Ridley was a committee member who had played a few non-first-class games for the county with conspicuous lack of success. The 1891 census shows that Bunny and Bessie lived in some comfort, with her sister and three servants. After selling Loseberry, his mother and sister moved to Scravels, a large house in Broomfield, close to Bunny. His mother died there in 1902, aged 86.

In 1892 the King Edward VI Grammar School moved from its cramped premises at Duke Street in Chelmsford to a new site next door to Westfield. The school took over Westfield for use as a preparatory school in 1924 which was the year after Lucas's death, but he moved away around 1902 so that was presumably a coincidence.

The Lucases were still at Westfield in 1901, but a year or two later the rector of Fryerning left the parish. The new rector chose to live in the

*Lucas's grave*

neighbouring town of Ingatestone, leaving the Rectory vacant and Bunny and Bessie moved in.[103] Two of their three servants – cook/housekeeper Ellen Heard and maid Millicent Fairchild – went with them and stayed until 1911 at least, so evidently there was loyalty on both sides.[104]

The rectory belonged not to the Kortrights, but to the lords of the manor, the Warden and Fellows of Wadham College Oxford, so Charles and his family cannot have given Lucas his home in Fryerning, though they may have pulled a few strings. Lucas was almost immediately elected a churchwarden. The rectory was set in five acres in an idyllic spot backing on to the churchyard, so he would not have had to go too far to carry out his duties. Already old in 1610, the house 'had been much altered and added to at various times [and] much improved of late years by painting the window-frames a dark colour, and encouraging the growth of creepers.'[105] It has since been replaced by a new building.[106]

The Lucases moved in 1916 to Brora, a house in Ingatestone on the corner of Roman Road and Avenue Road. Although it had only a small garden, its rateable value was slightly higher than that of the Fryerning rectory,[107] perhaps because it was only a short walk from the railway station and access to the City. It was also more modern and so altogether more convenient for the couple, who were now in their late fifties.

Around the end of 1922 they moved again, to The Cottage in the hamlet of Howe Street at Great Waltham, some four miles north of Chelmsford.[108] This move is more puzzling, because it took Lucas further away from his beloved Fryerning and there was no station in the village. It was apparently a more modest home, and he may have had to take it on as a result of losses

---

103    Essex annual reports give his address as Chelmsford in 1902 and Fryerning in 1903.
104    Censuses of 1901, 1911.
105    Wilde, E.E., *Ingatestone and the Essex Great Road with Fryerning*, Oxford University Press, 1913, pp 282-283.
106    Information from Robin Hobbs.
107    Inland Revenue finance book, 1910, Nos. 356 and 369, ERO A/R 2/3/20.
108    The Lucases are listed at Brora on the electoral register dated 14 October 1922, but not in Ingatestone or in Great Waltham after that. The Cottage is hardly a very distinctive name, and I have not been able to establish exactly where it was.

with the North-West Corporation. Sadly, Lucas did not have long to enjoy it, for he died there, suddenly, on 12 October 1923.

Lucas had continued to serve as a churchwarden in Fryerning and his funeral took place there four days later. Among the mourners were Charles Kortright and his brother William; Frank Penn, who toured Australia with Lucas in 1878/79; C.E.Ridley, his Uppingham Rovers team-mate and former landlord; and S.S.Storey, formerly Schultz, Lucas's lifelong colleague in the cricket field and on the Stock Exchange, who had to change his surname as a result of anti-German sentiment in World War I. There were also representatives of various organisations Lucas had been involved with, including MCC, Essex County Cricket Club, the Gentlemen of Essex, Chelmsford Cricket Club and the wardens of Chelmsford Cathedral.

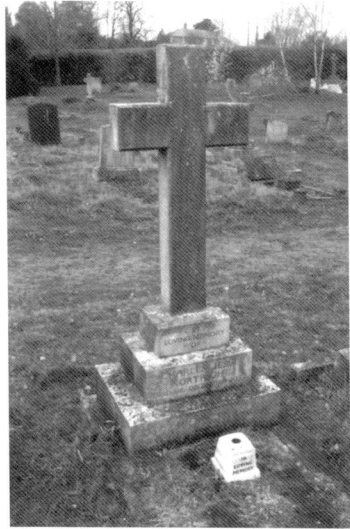

*Kortright's grave*

It was a tribute to Lucas that, when Charles Kortright died almost thirty years later, he chose to be buried not in the grand family vault next to the church but in a humble grave close to his old friend. And for Lucas, there could have been no more appropriate resting-place than a quiet country churchyard in the county where he made the second half of his life.

# *Acknowledgements*

Writing can be a solitary occupation, so I'm grateful to everyone who helped me along the way. David Jeater of the Association of Cricket Statisticians and Historians initially encouraged me, during the long journey to Derby for an ACS meeting, to think about writing the book. Then, as editor of the *Lives in Cricket* series, he gave constructive suggestions and unfailing support from the first draft to the final version.

The ACS were generous in giving me a grant that covered some of my expenses in researching the book. David Ashworth, President of the Uppingham Rovers, kindly allowed me to see the *Doings of the Uppingham Rovers* which, more than any other source, brought Bunny Lucas alive as a human being and a cricketer; he showed great hospitality, and was very patient in answering my many questions. Robin Hobbs provided a moving foreword and gave me a guided tour of Fryerning.

Thanks also, for their help in various ways, to Philip Bailey, Mike Boyers, Richard Cooper, Tony Debenham, Janice Eastment and Kevin Shaw, Pete Griffiths, Martin Hagger, Tom Hagger, Gerald Hudd, Pat Jeater, Howard Mallinson, Marilyn Mason, Douglas Miller, Dr Veronica Park, Zahra Ridge, Dr Phil Stevens, Jon Vallerius, my former colleagues at Vestry House Museum in Walthamstow, and the staff of Cambridge University Library, Essex Library Services, the Essex Record Office, the Lords Museum, the National Archives, the Society of Genealogists and the Surrey Heritage Centre.

The illustrations are reproduced by courtesy of Essex Record Office; Roger Mann; Malcolm Peebles; the Peter Edwards Museum and Library at Essex County Cricket Club; Roy Storey, Robin Hobbs and St Mary's Church, Fryerning; Uppingham Rovers Cricket Club and their president, David Ashworth; and Vestry House Museum, London Borough of Waltham Forest.

Nazeing, Essex
January, 2010

# Bibliography

The following are the main sources used in this life of Bunny Lucas:

*Australian Dictionary of Biography* online
*Bell's Life of London* magazine, 1874-1885
Bettesworth, W.A., *Chats on the Cricket Field,* Merritt and Hatcher, 1910
Birley, Derek, *A Social History of English Cricket*, Aurum, 1999
Bray, Charles, *Essex County Cricket*, Convoy, 1950
Brooke, Robert, *The Cricketer Book of Cricket Milestones*, Marks and Spencer, 1987
Censuses, 1841 to 1911
Cowley, Brian (ed), *Surrey County Cricket Club: First–Class Records, 1846–2000*, Surrey County Cricket Club, 2001
*Cricket* magazine, 1882-1914
*Cricket Field* magazine, 1892-1895
CricketArchive website
*The Doings of the Uppingham Rovers, 1863–* , first three of seven volumes, privately produced by the club
Essex County Cricket Club administrative records, housed at the Essex Record Office.
   [All the club items have the ERO prefix D/Z 82. The administrative records are numbered /1, and the relevant items have the following suffixes: *Committee minutes. 1*: 1886-93; *2*: 1893-1900; *35*: 1900-1908; *3*:1907-13. *Annual reports*: 6/1-155. *Scorebooks* are numbered /2 to /10.]
*Essex Chronicle* newspaper
Essex County Cricket Club, *Yearbooks*
FreeBMD website
Frindall, Bill, *The Wisden Book of Cricket Records* [Fourth Edition], Headline, 1998
Hawke, Lord, Harris, Lord and Gordon, Sir Home (eds), *Memorial Biography of Dr W.G. Grace*, Constable, 1919
Heald, Brian, *Essex County Cricket Club: First–Class Records, 1894–1994*, Limlow Books, 1995
*Kelly's London and Essex directories*
Lemmon, David and Marshall, Mike, *Essex County Cricket Club: The Official History*, Kingswood Press, 1986
Lemmon, David, *The Book of Essex Cricketers*, Breedon Books, 1994
*Leytonstone Express and Independent* newspaper
*John Lillywhite's Cricketers' Companion* annual, 1865-1985 ['Green Lilly']
*James Lillywhite's Cricketers' Annual,* 1872-1900 ['Red Lilly']

Mangan, J.A., *Athleticism in the Victorian and Edwardian Public School.*
    Cambridge University Press, 1981
Meredith, Anthony, *The Demon and The Lobster: Charles Kortright and
    Digby Jephson,* Kingswood Press, 1987
Patterson, W.S., *Sixty Years of Uppingham Cricket,* Longman, 1909
Rae, Simon, *W.G.Grace: A Life,* Faber, 1998
Royle, Vernon (with an introduction by Gerald Howat), *Lord Harris's
    Team in Australia 1878-79,* MCC / J.W.McKenzie, 2001
Sale, Charles, *Korty: The Legend Explained,* Ian Henry Publications, 1986
Stephenson, Roy, *H.H.Stephenson: A Cricketing Journey,* Uppingham
    Local History Study Group, 2009
*The Times* newspaper
*Walthamstow Guardian* newspaper
*Wisden Cricketer's Almanack* annual, 1864-1924

In addition to these, specific sources are footnoted throughout the text. In
some cases I have found information through internet sites which often
have very long addresses. Rather than reproduce them, I suggest that
readers wanting to follow up unfootnoted information may like to try an
internet search, always bearing in mind that these sources, like any other,
need careful evaluation. D.P.

# Appendix One
# Some Statistics

**Test cricket: Batting and Fielding**

|         | M | I | NO | R   | HS | Ave   | 100 | 50 | Ct |
|---------|---|---|----|-----|----|-------|-----|----|----|
| 1878/79 | 1 | 2 | 0  | 19  | 13 | 9.50  | -   | -  | -  |
| 1880    | 1 | 2 | 0  | 57  | 55 | 28.50 | -   | 1  | 1  |
| 1882    | 1 | 2 | 0  | 14  | 9  | 7.00  | -   | -  | -  |
| 1884    | 2 | 3 | 1  | 67  | 28 | 33.50 | -   | -  | -  |
| **Total** | **5** | **9** | **1** | **157** | **55** | **19.62** | **-** | **1** | **1** |

Notes: All Lucas' Test matches were against Australia, and all but his first in England. His highest Test score, 55, was in England's first innings at The Oval in 1880.

**Test cricket: Bowling**

|         | O  | M  | R  | W | BB | Ave | 5i |
|---------|----|----|----|---|----|-----|----|
| 1878/79 | 18 | 6  | 31 | 0 | -  | -   | -  |
| 1880    | 12 | 7  | 23 | 0 | -  | -   | -  |
| **Total** | **30** | **13** | **54** | **0** | **-** | **-** | **-** |

Notes: Lucas bowled in one innings in each of his first two Tests: overs were of four balls in both these games. He conceded runs at a rate equivalent to 2.70 per six-ball over.

**First-class cricket: Batting and Fielding**

|         | M  | I  | NO | R   | HS  | Ave   | 100 | 50 | Ct |
|---------|----|----|----|-----|-----|-------|-----|----|----|
| 1874    | 3  | 5  | 0  | 110 | 48  | 22.00 | -   | -  | 2  |
| 1875    | 13 | 22 | 2  | 440 | 63  | 22.00 | -   | 2  | 7  |
| 1876    | 16 | 30 | 3  | 818 | 105 | 30.29 | 1   | 5  | 5  |
| 1877    | 17 | 28 | 4  | 832 | 115 | 34.66 | 2   | 4  | 6  |
| 1878    | 16 | 27 | 1  | 522 | 91  | 20.07 | -   | 2  | 13 |
| 1878/79 | 5  | 9  | 1  | 158 | 51  | 19.75 | -   | 1  | 3  |
| 1879    | 10 | 18 | 1  | 423 | 70  | 24.88 | -   | 2  | 1  |
| 1880    | 11 | 20 | 0  | 353 | 66  | 17.65 | -   | 2  | 12 |
| 1881    | 14 | 27 | 2  | 712 | 142 | 28.48 | 1   | 2  | 13 |
| 1882    | 15 | 25 | 3  | 707 | 145 | 32.13 | 2   | 3  | 16 |
| 1883    | 12 | 23 | 3  | 664 | 97  | 33.20 | -   | 4  | 13 |
| 1884    | 9  | 17 | 1  | 263 | 37  | 16.43 | -   | -  | 4  |
| 1887    | 5  | 10 | 3  | 193 | 47  | 27.57 | -   | -  | 2  |
| 1888    | 3  | 5  | 0  | 94  | 50  | 18.80 | -   | 1  | 2  |
| 1889    | 1  | 2  | 0  | 20  | 17  | 10.00 | -   | -  | 1  |
| 1890    | 1  | 2  | 0  | 49  | 37  | 24.50 | -   | -  | -  |
| 1894    | 6  | 10 | 1  | 88  | 25  | 9.77  | -   | -  | 3  |
| 1895    | 4  | 6  | 0  | 175 | 135 | 29.16 | 1   | -  | -  |
| 1896    | 3  | 5  | 0  | 160 | 56  | 32.00 | -   | 1  | 2  |
| 1897    | 10 | 14 | 3  | 386 | 89  | 35.09 | -   | 4  | 6  |

| | | | | | | | | |
|---|---|---|---|---|---|---|---|---|
| 1898 | 13 | 19 | 3 | 472 | 89 | 29.50 | - | 2 | 6 |
| 1899 | 11 | 18 | 5 | 393 | 67 | 30.23 | - | 2 | 6 |
| 1900 | 15 | 21 | 1 | 626 | 95 | 31.30 | - | 5 | 3 |
| 1901 | 15 | 26 | 6 | 742 | 83 | 37.10 | - | 6 | 11 |
| 1902 | 11 | 17 | 1 | 438 | 103 | 27.37 | 1 | 2 | 6 |
| 1903 | 9 | 15 | 1 | 174 | 49 | 12.42 | - | - | 4 |
| 1904 | 3 | 5 | 0 | 68 | 44 | 13.60 | - | - | 4 |
| 1905 | 2 | 4 | 1 | 67 | 34 | 22.33 | - | - | - |
| 1906 | 1 | 2 | 0 | 67 | 34 | 33.50 | - | - | - |
| 1907 | 2 | 3 | 0 | 49 | 49 | 16.33 | - | - | 1 |
| **Total** | **256** | **435** | **46** | **10263** | **145** | **26.38** | **8** | **50** | **152** |

*Notes: Apart from five matches in Australia in 1878/79, Lucas played all his first-class cricket in England. He did not appear in first-class cricket in the seasons 1885, 1886 and 1891 to 1893. He was dismissed 183 times bowled (47%); 176 times caught (45%); 20 times run out (5%); six times lbw (2%); three times stumped (1%) and hit wicket once. The three bowlers who took his wicket most often were F.Morley 17, A.Shaw 14 and W.G.Grace 13.*

### First-class cricket: Bowling

| | | *O* | *M* | *R* | *W* | *BB* | *Ave* | *5i* |
|---|---|---|---|---|---|---|---|---|
| 1874 | (4-b) | 13 | 1 | 54 | 2 | 2-41 | 27.00 | - |
| 1876 | (4-b) | 30 | 6 | 64 | 0 | - | - | - |
| 1877 | (4-b) | 373.2 | 176 | 470 | 34 | 5-50 | 13.82 | 1 |
| 1878 | (4-b) | 314 | 153 | 363 | 22 | 5-34 | 16.50 | 1 |
| 1878/79 | (4-b) | 239.1 | 105 | 347 | 14 | 3-32 | 24.78 | - |
| 1879 | (4-b) | 97 | 42 | 117 | 8 | 3-22 | 14.62 | - |
| 1880 | (4-b) | 261.1 | 117 | 358 | 23 | 5-23 | 15.56 | 1 |
| 1881 | (4-b) | 185 | 63 | 320 | 16 | 4-40 | 20.00 | - |
| 1882 | (4-b) | 247.3 | 92 | 386 | 26 | 6-10 | 14.84 | 1 |
| 1883 | (4-b) | 45 | 13 | 89 | 2 | 1-17 | 44.50 | - |
| 1884 | (4-b) | 39 | 9 | 89 | 4 | 2-34 | 22.25 | - |
| 1887 | (4-b) | 37 | 11 | 63 | 0 | - | - | - |
| 1888 | (4-b) | 5 | 2 | 7 | 2 | 2-7 | 3.50 | - |
| 1890 | (5-b) | 30 | 12 | 32 | 1 | 1-5 | 32.00 | - |
| 1894 | (5-b) | 3 | 0 | 15 | 0 | - | - | - |
| 1898 | (5-b) | 2 | 0 | 17 | 1 | 1-17 | 17.00 | - |
| 1900 | (6-b) | 15 | 1 | 58 | 0 | - | - | - |
| **Total** | **(4-b)** | **1885.3** | **790** | | | | | |
| | **(5-b)** | **35** | **12** | **2849** | **155** | **6-10** | **18.38** | **4** |
| | **(6-b)** | **15** | **1** | | | | | |

*Notes: Lucas bowled in 96 of his 256 first-class matches, and took wickets in 56 of them. He took his wickets at the rate of one per 50.37 balls and conceded runs at a rate equivalent to 2.18 per six-ball over. 87 (56%) of his dismissals were caught; 57 (37%) were bowled; seven (5%) were stumped; two (1%) were hit wicket, and two (1%) were lbw. He dismissed three batsmen more than three times: these were F.Morley 5, H.Jupp and Richard Daft, both 4.*

### First-class cricket: Centuries (8)

| Score | For | Opponent | Venue | Season |
|---|---|---|---|---|
| 105 | Cambridge Univ[1] | England XI | Fenner's | 1876 |
| 115 | Surrey[1] | Nottinghamshire | The Oval | 1877 |
| 110 | Surrey[1] | Kent | Maidstone | 1877 |
| 142 | Gents of England[1] | Cambridge Univ | Fenner's | 1881 |
| 145 | England XI[1] | Cambridge Univ | Fenner's | 1882 |

| | | | | |
|---|---|---|---|---|
| 107 | Gentlemen[1] | Players | Lord's | 1882 |
| 135 | Essex[1] | Somerset | Taunton | 1895 |
| 103 | Essex[1] | Derbyshire | Leyton | 1902 |

*Note: Lucas was dismissed caught in all eight of these innings.*

## First-Class cricket: Five wickets or more in an innings (4)

| Bowling | For | Opponent | Venue | Season |
|---|---|---|---|---|
| 37-16-50-5 | Surrey | Nottinghamshire[2] | The Oval | 1877 |
| 32-16-34-5 | Cambridge Univ | Gents of England[1] | Fenner's | 1878 |
| 14-4-23-5 | Surrey | Gloucestershire[2] | The Oval | 1880 |
| 12.2-5-10-6 | England XI | Cambridge Univ[2] | Fenner's | 1882 |

*Notes: Overs were of four balls in all these matches. Lucas' highest score and his best bowling return were in the same match.*

## Matches for Essex 1889-1893: Batting and Fielding

| | M | I | NO | R | HS | Ave | 100 | 50 | Ct/St |
|---|---|---|---|---|---|---|---|---|---|
| 1889 | 6 | 10 | 1 | 334 | 103 | 37.11 | 1 | - | 4 |
| 1890 | 8 | 14 | 2 | 268 | 55 | 22.33 | - | 1 | - |
| 1891 | 6 | 10 | 1 | 315 | 113 | 35.00 | 1 | - | 7/1 |
| 1892 | 7 | 13 | 2 | 347 | 74 | 31.54 | - | 3 | 5/1 |
| 1893 | 10 | 16 | 3 | 599 | 175 | 46.07 | 1 | 4 | 1 |
| **Total** | **37** | **63** | **9** | **1863** | **175** | **34.50** | **3** | **9** | **17/2** |

## Matches for Essex 1889-1893: Bowling

| | O | M | R | W | BB | Ave | 5i |
|---|---|---|---|---|---|---|---|
| 1889 | 66 | 20 | 140 | 5 | 3-51 | 28.00 | - |
| 1890 | 21 | 3 | 75 | 2 | 2-19 | 37.50 | - |
| 1891 | 57 | 16 | 112 | 4 | 2-45 | 28.00 | - |
| 1892 | 7 | 0 | 35 | 1 | 1-4 | 35.00 | - |
| **Total** | **151** | **39** | **362** | **12** | **3-51** | **30.16** | **-** |

*Notes: Overs were of five balls in all these seasons. Lucas did not bowl in 1893.*

## Matches for Essex 1889-1893: Centuries (8)

| Score | For | Opponent | Venue | Season |
|---|---|---|---|---|
| 103 | Essex[1] | MCC | Leyton | 1889 |
| 113 | Essex[1] | Warwickshire | Edgbaston | 1891 |
| 175 | Essex[1] | Hampshire | Leyton | 1893 |

*Note: The index figures [1] and [2] in this and preceding tables indicate the innings in which the feat was achieved.*

Sources: cricketarchive.com and Wisden Cricketers' Almanack.

# Appendix Two
## The only tied Gentlemen v Players match

GENTLEMEN v PLAYERS
Played at Kennington Oval, June 28, 28, 30, 1883.
Match tied.

### PLAYERS

| | | | | | |
|---|---|---|---|---|---|
| 1 R.G.Barlow | b Steel | 47 | c Forbes b Steel | | 31 |
| 2 G.Ulyett | c Kemp b Steel | 63 | c and b Rotherham | | 10 |
| 3 A.Shrewsbury | b Studd | 11 | (4) b Steel | | 0 |
| 4 E.Lockwood | b Rotherham | 18 | (5) b Steel | | 8 |
| 5 W.Barnes | c Steel b Rotherham | 20 | (6) st Kemp b Steel | | 28 |
| 6 W.Robinson | c Forbes b Studd | 8 | (7) c and b Steel | | 6 |
| 7 W.Bates | not out | 19 | (3) b Frank | | 76 |
| 8 W.Flowers | c and b Rotherham | 0 | c Lucas b Steel | | 7 |
| 9 T.Emmett | b Rotherham | 8 | b Steel | | 0 |
| 10 E.Peate | b Rotherham | 0 | c and b Frank | | 3 |
| 11 +M.Sherwin | b Rotherham | 3 | not out | | 2 |
| Extras | (1 b, 5 lb) | 6 | (4 b, 6 lb) | | 10 |
| Total | | 203 | | | 181 |

FoW (1): 1-92, 2-123, 3-125, 4-154, 5-171, 6-173, 7-181, 8-199, 9-199, 10-203
FoW (2): 1-30, 2-77, 3-77, 4-89, 5-152, 6-165, 7-170, 8-170, 9-173, 10-181

### GENTLEMEN

| | | | | | |
|---|---|---|---|---|---|
| 1 Lord Harris | b Bates | 38 | (4) b Barlow | | 0 |
| 2 A.P.Lucas | run out | 8 | not out | | 47 |
| 3 C.T.Studd | c Sherwin b Emmett | 30 | c Robinson b Emmett | | 20 |
| 4 C.W.Wright | c Bates b Barlow | 21 | (5) b Emmett | | 1 |
| 5 *A.N.Hornby | run out | 20 | (1) c Shrewsbury b Flowers | | 11 |
| 6 A.G.Steel | b Barnes | 21 | lbw b Flowers | | 31 |
| 7 W.F.Forbes | c Lockwood b Barnes | 28 | c Shrewsbury b Flowers | | 4 |
| 8 +M.C.Kemp | b Barlow | 6 | (9) c Barlow b Flowers | | 2 |
| 9 C.F.H.Leslie | lbw b Barnes | 12 | (8) c Shrewsbury b Flowers | | 5 |
| 10 J.Frank | b Flowers | 16 | b Flowers | | 6 |
| 11 H.Rotherham | not out | 13 | b Peate | | 11 |
| Extras | (19 b, 2 lb, 1 w) | 22 | (7 b, 4 lb) | | 11 |
| Total | | 235 | | | 149 |

FoW (1): 1-42, 2-52, 3-93, 4-130, 5-135, 6-178, 7-189, 8-195, 9-214, 10-235
FoW (2): 1-18, 2-49, 3-49, 4-50, 5-92, 6-99, 7-104, 8-115, 9-136, 10-149

Gentlemen Bowling

|  | O | M | R | W |  | O | M | R | W |
|---|---|---|---|---|---|---|---|---|---|
| Studd | 42 | 16 | 67 | 2 |  | 18 | 7 | 38 | 0 |
| Rotherham | 25.2 | 8 | 41 | 6 |  | 18 | 2 | 54 | 1 |
| Steel | 40 | 23 | 56 | 2 |  | 26 | 10 | 43 | 7 |
| Frank | 5 | 1 | 15 | 0 |  | 12 | 8 | 12 | 2 |
| Forbes | 19 | 12 | 18 | 0 |  | 12 | 4 | 24 | 0 |

Players Bowling

|  | O | M | R | W |  | O | M | R | W |
|---|---|---|---|---|---|---|---|---|---|
| Peate | 34 | 17 | 39 | 0 |  | 30.2 | 16 | 26 | 1 |
| Barlow | 34 | 13 | 37 | 2 |  | 23 | 11 | 26 | 1 |
| Barnes | 28 | 13 | 48 | 3 |  | 18 | 7 | 29 | 0 |
| Bates | 22 | 12 | 33 | 1 |  |  |  |  |  |
| Ulyett | 14 | 7 | 21 | 0 |  | 4 | 2 | 7 | 0 |
| Emmett | 8 | 3 | 18 | 1 |  | 7 | 5 | 10 | 2 |
| Flowers | 11.2 | 5 | 17 | 1 |  | 44 | 24 | 40 | 6 |

Umpires: H Jupp, J Street.          Toss: Players

Close of Play: 1st day: Gentlemen (1) 92-3 (Wright 11*); 2nd day: Players (2) 181 all out.

Source: cricketarchive.com

# Index

A page number in bold indicates an illustration.

Penn, Frank **46**, 50, 51, 53, 56, 125
Perkins, Henry  44
Perrin, P.A.  **100**, 102, 103, 113, 117, 118, 121
Pickett, Henry  90, 94, 97, 99, 100, **100**, 101
Pilling, Richard  57
Plumer, R.S.  39
Prince's Cricket Ground, Chelsea  23, 37

Raffles, A.J.  20, 21
Ranjitsinhji, K.S.  109
Rawnsley, Canon H.D.  16
Read, A.H.  81
Read, H.D. ('Hopper')  81
Read, W.W.  **66**
Reeves, William  105-107
Repton School  16, 19
Rhodes, Wilfred  107
Rhyming Rover  23, 24, 29, 30
Rickling Green, Essex  57, 58, 117fn
Ridley, A.W.  39
Ridley, C.E.  24, 119, 123, 125
Robertson, William  48
Robinson, G.E.  58
Roller, W.E.  **67**
Rolls, Hon C.S.  37
Rossall School, Fleetwood  17
Rotherham, Hugh  27, 29, 31, 63, 81
Round, Rt Hon James, MP  88
Royal Commission on the Stock Exchange, 1878  69-70
Royle, V.P.F.A.  46-54, 76
Russell, C.A.G. ('Jack')  95
Russell, T.M. ('Tom')  94, 95, **96**, 99-103, 110, 121
Rylott, Arnold  37

St George's C.C., Hoboken  54
St Kilda, Victoria  47, 52
St Mary's church, Fryerning  5, 8, 54, 74, 76, 120
Salmon, Elizabeth Frederica (Lucas's grandmother)  10, 13
Salmon, William Orton (Lucas's grandfather)  11
San Francisco, California  53
Schultz (later Storey), S.S.  7, 22, 33, 46, **46**, 48, 49, 57, 70, 83, 125
Schwarz, R.O.  111
Second-class counties  88, 89, 91-93, 97
Sedgwick, G.A.  112
Sewell, E.H.D.  109
Shadwell, F.B.  26
Shaw, Alfred  37, 130

Shrewsbury, Arthur  65, **66**, 82
Smith, Sir C.Aubrey  29
Smith, T.P.B.  99
Somerset C.C.C.  89, 99
Sonning, Berkshire  13
South [of England team]  63, 66
South African (Boer) War  21, 105
South Africans (tourists)  111
South Australia  47
Southern Tasmania Cricket Association  49
Spofforth, F.R.  5, 49, 50, 60, 65, 66
Staffordshire, Gentlemen of  24
Staffordshire C.C.C.  91
Staten Island C.C. New York  54
Steel, A.G.  35, **43**, 44, 63, 65, 66, **66**, **67**, 79
Steel, D.Q.  7, 24, 40, **43**, 82, 85
Steel, H.B.  **67**
Stephenson, H.H.  7, 16, 17, 18, **18**, 19-22, 31, 33, 35, 37, 56 82, 95, 121
Stewart, Prof James  38
Stock Exchange  8, 35, 69-73, 101, 125
Stoddart, A.E.  **100**
Strachan, George  55
Streatfeild, E.C.  91
Studd, C.T.  60, 63
Studd, J.E.K.  **67**
Sugg, F.H.  111
Surrey C.C.C.  7, 37-44, 55-63, 65, 70, 86, 89-93, 96, 97, 101-104, 107, 113
'Surrey Veteran, A'  58, 60
Sussex, Gentlemen of  27
Sussex C.C.C.  56, 76, 105, 106, 110
Sutthery, A.M.  86
Sydney, New South Wales  49-53

Taberer, H.M.  81, 95
Tasmania  49
Taunton, County Ground  99
Taylor, T.L  107
Tebbut, C.M.  94, 101
Test matches  48-9, 56, 60-61, 65, 66, **66**, 83, 85, 108
Thornton, C.I  38, 57, 58, 68
Thorpe-le-Soken, Essex  77
Thring, Edward  16-18
Tonbridge School, Kent  11, 16, 120
Tooting C.C.  23
Townsend, C.L.  **100**
Trevor, E.H.  58
Trollope, Anthony: *The Way We Live Now*  69
Trott, G.H.S. ('Harry')  91
Trumble, Hugh  96, 103, 104, 109